SET

THE CAPTIVES

FREE

CW00402585

Chima Ugochukwu

© 2015 Chima Ugochukwu
First Published August, 2015
ISBN: 9781098749279

ALL RIGHTS RESERVED

No portion of this publication may be
translated into any language or repro-duced in
any form, except for brief quotations in reviews
without prior written permission of the author
and publisher.

NOTE: All Scripture quotations are from the
Authorized King James Version of the HOLY
BIBLE

DEDICATION

This work is dedicated to the director general of the military church of our lord jesus christ, the wonderful holy spirit and one of god's special generals, rev. Dr. Uma ukpai (the apostle of miracles) and his dear wife, pastor (mrs.) Philomena uma ukpai

Their parental blessings, prayers, and guidance to my family and Ministry are inestimable.

ACKNOWLEDGEMENTS

I appreciate and acknowledge great ministers of God, whose works have influenced me and my writings in many ways.

I immensely acknowledge and appreciate that the works and teachings of Dr. Abraham Chigbundu and Gomba Fortune Oyor, among others, have influenced my writings and works on deliverance. Your oils are in this work.

I seriously appreciate the most beautiful woman in the world, the wife of my youth, for her prayers and support.

I also appreciate Prof. (Mrs.) Nkechinyere Nwokoye, Pastor (Mrs.) Ebere Chiemerie, and Anulika Oduenyi for reading through the work.

Finally, I appreciate my daughters: Ifedigbo Chinenye, Ugochukwu Peace, and Ugochukwu Ozioma for typing and arranging the manuscript.

~ Canon Chima Ugochukwu

FOREWORD

Perusing through this book, it is termed a masterpiece; it came at a time when the world is decaying and many believers are stranded due to afflictions of life. In a time when evil is on the increase and many yield to the yarning of the devil, whereby they knowingly or unknowingly became prey in the hand of the adversary. Therefore, it is pertinent to say that this book is a must read for every Christian.

Deliverance perhaps, is the most difficult and dangerous aspect of Christian ministry, hence, it deals with rescuing the captives whether lawful or not. Rev. Canon Chima deemed it fit at this point to delve into lawful captives. Many are captives without their knowledge and they are going down spiritually on daily basis. Many Christians are suffering in the hand of the devil and without deliverance, they cannot excel. Therefore, this masterpiece x-rays the signs and symptoms of demonic presence, many ways one can become a lawful captive, and different ways one can attract curses and varying degrees of evil covenants.

However, Rev. Canon Chima in this masterpiece gave assurance to all Christians that through Christ, deliverance is assured in his concerted effort to showcase the supremacy of God over Satan. Chapter one is full of assurance of deliverance from God no matter the gravity of demons, curses, captivity, and covenants one finds himself. The power of God over Satan, demons, curses, captivity, sickness, and troubles was made manifest.

In chapters 2, 3, and 4, demonic presence, how one can become a lawful captive, and how people attract curses were enumerated and dealt with in details. The three chapters opened my eyes to many things I did not know. Chapters 5 and 6 x-rayed covenants, varying degrees/types of covenants, and how one can be a lawful captive through covenants. Covenants have kept many believers aback for centuries and they have prayed all kinds and manners of prayer to no avail. But, this book is an answer.

I strongly believe that with this rich knowledge of the deliverance concept, there would be a diminution in the prevalence and impact of freedom for all Christians. Therefore, I regard this book as a guide to achieving the ultimate desired hope of His (God's) calling for all believers in this changing world, and I am happy to be associated with it.

Rev. Onyeachulam Sylvanus
Supervisor, Special Duties (SSD),
Post Primary Schools Service Commission,
Onitsha Zone, Anambra State, Nigeria.

TABLE OF CONTENTS

CHAPTER ONE

THERE SHALL BE DELIVERANCE

So many believers and even ministers are going through horrible experiences that cannot be explained humanly or naturally. In most cases, these experiences are so real and very much in existence that they interrupt the person's normal existence. Horribly, some people have this encounter at the spirit realm and are the only people that can tell the tale while to some others, the spiritual encounter proceeds to the physical, causing havoc to the person and to people around.

Most often, when this encounter begins to manifest physically, some take to conventional methods as means of solving the problem. Eventually, the use of conventional method tends to worsen the situation rather than granting the desired solution. Why? - It takes a mystery to dissolve the mysterious. You do not solve a mysterious problem through conventional methods.

Explicitly, it has been established through experiences and even Biblical reports that some problems that defy conventional methods require simple prayer of deliverance. WHY? - Some of these problems have spirits supervising them, and some of these spirits are contacted through personal involvement in some things, family, or ancestral involvement. This goes to say that some of these spirits (who oppress their victims with sickness, madness, or strange experiences), have legal holds on their victims, and oppress them on that stand. If they must be dislodged, it must involve the ministry of "lose him and let him go" or some levels of renunciations in the case of covenants. This is referred to as DELIVERANCE.

Talking about deliverance, the Bible reveals through the Gospel that every time Jesus sent out His disciples to preach, He also commanded them to cast out devils. The ministry of casting out devils simply talks about deliverance. This can be seen in the following Bible passages:

"And when he had called unto him his twelve disciples, he gave them power against unclean spirits, to cast them out, and to heal all manner of sickness and all manner of disease. And as ye go, preach, saying, The kingdom of heaven is at hand. Heal the sick, cleanse the lepers, raise the dead, CAST OUT DEVILS: freely ye have received, freely give." – Matthew 10: 1, 7-8

"And he ordained twelve, that they should be with him, and that he might send them forth to preach. And to have power to heal sicknesses, and to CAST OUT DEVILS." – Mark 3:14-15

"And they went out, and preached that men should repent. And they CAST OUT MANY DEVILS, and anointed with oil many that were sick, and healed them." – Mark 6:12-13

"And He said to them, Go you into all the world and preach the gospel to every creature. He that believes and is baptized shall be saved: but he that believes not shall be damned. And these signs shall follow them that believe. In My Name shall they CAST OUT DEVILS: they shall speak with new tongues. They shall take up serpents: and if they drink any deadly thing, it shall not hurt them, they shall lay hands on the sick, and they shall recover." – Mark 16:15-18

These are only a few examples for this discussion. See my book "THIS IS DELIVERANCE" for details.

Disappointedly, a lot of people have been taught by some ministers that deliverance is not necessary and they believed it. But the question is: "Do these ministers confusing people about deliverance have a different Bible? Are they truly for God or against God?"

It is good you know that Biblical evidences make it very obvious that anybody teaching against deliverance is operating in ignorance, which has the capacity to (not only) destroy them, but also their followers. This is because the battle is very real, and these issues have no respect for title or age. Also, the spirits involved can reduce men to animal level when they are not properly handled. That is why you need adequate knowledge and not arguing against evidence. Recall that the Bible says: "My people perish for lack of knowledge."

However, I am not in any way saying that every minister must become a deliverance minister. No! If deliverance is not your calling, keep quiet. Stop destroying the faith of others.

It is very painful to say that a lot of believers have moved from believing churches/fellowships into fetish practices because of their pastor/priest's teachings. Some even died. A typical example is the case of a sister, who was working in a believers' ministry for more than seven years. She started hearing strange voices and was advised to go for deliverance. But the ministry's leadership refused, saying that they do not believe in it. They also said that they were praying about it their own way. The result was that the spirit oppressed and dominated this humble (obedient) sister until she committed suicide in her room out of frustration.

PAINFUL EXPERIENCES

Indeed people go through a lot of experiences. It can be in the case of marital problems that have strange explanations; strange experiences that often occur in dreams, business failures, and the like. Some of such experiences require immediate spiritual attention through deliverance. Sorting such individuals out (via deliverance) may be all that there is to their liberation from such experiences.

Some years ago, I met a sister, who reported that she never stayed in any marriage above eleven months. She kept marrying and divorcing. The question is: Why is she being divorced incessantly? She had a simple case that would have been sorted out through deliverance, but because of the erroneous teaching she received and believed, the case had gained her pains and shame that she did not bargain.

However, while we dealt with her case, we discovered that it was simply a marine husband (very jealous spirit husband) that did not want to share her with anybody. The demon dealt so much with her irrespective of time and space. According to her, the last guy that married her took her to South Africa, thinking that the demons would not cross the river. Yet the demons came there and took her away, and by the time she was coming into Nigeria, the fourth husband was already hanging around. But she was worried about what the case would be if she marries again. Also, she was considering what the elders would say having asked whether she would be able to stay if they should accept another man. This exactly was what made her to agree to deliverance.

Consider what she had been through because of simple wrong gospel preached by a minister, which she believed: The pains and the price she paid for such wrong gospel. Painfully, the people that preached the wrong gospel that she accepted had gone their way without knowing the pains and the price she had paid for it.

Do you know how many people whose businesses have collapsed because they married a lady who is married to one useless demon, (who is a principality)? These demons are so jealous that they are not willing to relinquish or let go of their claimed wives. They can deal with you and everything around you with which you take care of her to the point that you become incapable of taking care of her. Funnily, when they raze-down all you have, they also come to supervise your quarrels with her.

Again, it is good you know that deliverance is not for sisters alone. Brothers also need deliverance. I have handled a case with some brethren in one of our prayer conferences. While the conference was on, a sister was brought with an astonishing and complicating case. This sister could neither talk nor blink her eyes. She could neither sleep nor eat for three days. She was only moping or gazing without blinking for three days. What was the problem? The spirit wife of the husband slapped the devil out of her for interfering and meddling too much in the marriage. While the problem lasted, the spirit wife took over, because in that state, she could not do much of marriage requirements.

In another instance, a married woman complained to me that her marriage was on fire. The sister said that any day the husband tried touching her, he would sleep outside the house without knowing until morning. Why? - The spirit husband of the woman used to make sure that he was carried outside (unknowing) while the doors were locked. The man only gets to realize that he slept on grasses (outside the house) early in the morning, when the spirit husband had finished sleeping with his wife.

Surprisingly, despite all these evidences, some still argue against deliverance. They anchor their arguments on the premises that he that is in Christ Jesus is a new creature, old things have passed away. Indeed everything has become new. I like to ask, "Does it include un-renounced marriage covenant with spirit husband/wife, unbroken ancestral covenants and dedications, un-renounced (unknown) initiations to idolatry with spirits who work on legal grounds?" I mean, name it. It is really terrible.

In the case presented, although she is a new creature in Christ and old things had indeed passed away, the spirit husbands were still oppressing her because she had not been sorted out through deliverance. Go and read the scripture again. When Jesus came to Lazarus, who had been in the grave for three days, He looked at him. Remember that Lazarus was dead already. After some time, He shouted with a loud voice and ordered him to come forth, and according to the Bible, at His command, Lazarus came back to life.

But there was something Jesus saw, which others did not see. Jesus knew that even though Lazarus was alive, he could not go far. He would not be able to run a hundred meters race. His life could only move like that of a tortoise, because he was bound (head, hand, and toe) with graveyard clothes. And Jesus said: "Loose him and let him go." Then he that was bound was loosed.

Like Lazarus, many born again believers are walking around with graveyard clothes, and they need the ministry of Loose-him-and-let-him-go. Have you gone through it? Are you walking around with graveyard clothes and telling us that you are born again? Please go to be sorted out.

According to the Bible, every unbeliever who has not accepted Jesus as his personal Lord and Saviour is already dead like Lazarus in the graveyard, rapped and bound. Just like the sisters of Lazarus, their people are worried because they are always drinking, smoking, womanizing, and are wasting their lives here and there. This lifestyle gives Satan right over them. But when they get born again, everybody rejoices, like they rejoiced when Lazarus came back to life. The people were excited and they rejoiced. But until they are sorted out, they are like Lazarus bound and wrapped with graveyard clothes, which limit how far they can go in life's endeavours.

Indeed, deliverance is one endeavour that every Christian, whose interest is to serve God (righteously without camouflage) and enjoy the dividend of serving God, should embark on. It is like the issuance of keys to a building after accepting the occupancy of that building. It is a never overlooked or ignored aspect of Christian living.

Talking about the importance of deliverance and God's readiness/provision through deliverance to any man that submits himself for deliverance, Obadiah 1:17 says:

"But on Mount Zion there shall be deliverance, and there shall be holiness; and the house of Jacob shall possess their possession."

In this Scripture, there are three definite factors, which are intertwined – deliverance, holiness, and possessing of possession. The Bible made it clear that on this mountain, there shall be deliverance, after which comes holiness. The question is: Why will there by deliverance before holiness? Deliverance is required to attain a holy life. Without deliverance, living holy will become a struggle. X-raying on this, the Bible records that all the Christians in the Corinthian church were struggling to live holy. Although they were born again, and were prophesying and raising the dead, the Bible says that they were not just committing immorality, but, they were sleeping with their father's wives.

This is exactly the picture. So many Christians are struggling to live holy because of spirits that inhabit them. For example, a sister was brought to our ministry. The sister had been born again for about thirteen years. She is filled with the Holy Ghost and was working in a ministry/church where all that she was hearing was about the Bible, heaven, hell, etc., as a secretary for about seven years. But she was having a strange experience. According to her, sometimes when she was alone and everywhere is quiet, she would suddenly discover that her heart turns into a conference table. People would be discussing over her heart and she would be hearing the discussions and contributions of different people. These discussions were mostly on things that are filthy, dirty, and things that have nothing to do with Christianity. According to her, this experience was a regular one.

When I heard this story, it sounded very strange to me because I was still very young in ministry. But I was interested. So, I asked her to begin to plead the blood of Jesus continuously. I had asked her to plead the Blood of Jesus, because, the Bible says:

The Blood of Jesus purges our spirit, soul, and body and cleanses us from all unrighteousness.

At a point, I discovered a drop in the rate at which she was pleading the Blood of Jesus. She was almost finding it difficult to plead the Blood of Jesus, like it was when she started. Then I knew that something was wrong. I also knew that the spirit that would not allow her to plead the Blood of Jesus is not a good one. So I became more interested.

As the rate at which she was pleading the blood of Jesus dropped, she started saying "egedege" "egedege" (that is an Igbo local dance). Then I turned and said: I bind the spirit of "egedege" in the name of Jesus and asked her to open her eyes. When she did, she was looking like a person saved from drowning in the swimming pool. Then I asked her to tell me the business between her and egedege dance. She told me that it was during their secondary days, when they were preparing for the coming of one commissioner to their school. On this preparation, they were taught to dance 'egedege' as an entertainment for the expected commissioner. However, nobody knew that some egedege demons entered her. These spirits work in cluster – they do not walk alone.

Again, you need to understand that diversity exists in our backgrounds. Some backgrounds are more sophisticated than the others, because of the covenants, articles of the covenants, and dedication involved. Also, our exposures in life are not the same. Some people were involved in some practices that did not glorify God while some lived very immoral life as unbelievers. Thus, it is good to know that if you ever lived immorally in the world, you need deliverance to be able to live and keep the standard of God – holiness. This is because the Bible says that harlots are mistresses of witchcraft, and in witchcraft, a man initiates a woman and a woman vice versa. (This shows how much Satan has his plan perfectly arranged. It is not a matter or calculation of human sense).

Therefore, if you lived immoral life, enough demons had invaded you. You need to go through serious curse breaking. Why? - Curses can be exchanged through this adventurous act. I counseled a girl who said that she had slept with three hundred and ten different men, including Muslims, terrorists, etc. What do you think will happen if you sleep with this kind of person? How many curses do you think will be transferred or exchanged in one day? To understand it, get a bottle of neat water, and drop a small drop of coke into it. You will discover that the colour will change from being clear water to something else. The same happens, if you keep dropping different types of soft drinks like malt, Fanta, etc. That is the way different blood and spirits come. Yet people still claim that nothing has happened. May God have mercy on you.

Having said this, it is plausible to note that attaining a holy life and possession of possession requires deliverance from invaded spirits, whose duty is to limit how far you can go. Importantly, it is worthy of note to say that although a lot of people think that deliverance is about casting out demons, it goes deeper than casting out demons. The question is: What then is deliverance?

DEFINITIONS OF DELIVERANCE

Deliverance is the removal of Egypt out of the life of the man who has left the spiritual Egypt. Historically, Egypt can be likened to a place of bondage and slavery. Within Biblical reports, you often hear, "Abraham went down to Egypt." This shows that Egypt is a place of DOWN. When a man is not born again, he is in

Egypt. But, when he comes out of Egypt, he is born again. Now that he is born again, we need to remove the spiritual Egypt, (the graveyard clothes) out of his life. This indeed is very important.

In the case of Moses, God called him and wanted to use him to deliver his people. As at the time Moses was called, he was already forty years. As a result of the circumstances surrounding his birth and life as a toddler/newborn, Moses was trained in Pharaoh's palace. Even his name "Moses" came from the water. Looking through his family lineage, the anointing of anger and all kinds of things were discovered. The Bible says that suddenly, this man realized that the call of God was in his life. But he was in a hurry to serve God like many of us. Once they discover that God is calling them, they will no more be patient to go through training. They do not know that there is a distance between the CALL and the COMMISSION.

In his case, Moses hurriedly (without preparation) began to deliver the Israelites out of Egypt. Despite his zeal, his evil family pattern could not allow him to do it rightly. Having seen that Moses was at verge of destroying his ministry if he is not sorted out, God banished him out of Egypt and sent him to the wilderness for forty years. Within these forty years, God was conducting deliverance on Moses, to sort him out and to remove spiritual Egypt from him.

Moses' life in the wilderness is graphic enough, showing the importance of deliverance in the life of a believer. In 1 Corinthians 10:5, the Bible says something about all the men that left Egypt, without removing spiritual Egypt out of their lives. It says:

"But with most of them God was not well pleased, for their bodies were scattered in the wilderness."

What is the Bible saying? These were the mixed-multitude that left Egypt, whose vocal exhibitions/utterances showed greatly that their spirits were still tied to Egypt. Words such as: "Did we not tell you to leave us and to let us serve the Egyptians. Yet, you brought us here to suffer," were all indications that though they were out of Egypt, Egypt had not left them.

Many Christians are out of Egypt but Egypt has not left them. Deliverance will sort you out, removing the spiritual Egypt out of you, who is said to have left Egypt. For instance, casting out immoral spirits such as spirits of lust, seduction, impure thoughts, and sexual flash-backs gathered from pornography and ugly experiences requires adequate sorting out through deliverance.

Deliverance is the process of casting out evil spirits from their victims. The question is: who are these victims? These can be:

i.   Material Possession – I heard about a case where a cow went mad and was misbehaving. As a result, a conductor of a bus came out and spoke to the animal. The animal became quiet. Further, he said something again, which nobody heard, the animal went down on its four legs. The conductor entered his car and left. What does this show? A person's possession can be demonized and can be sorted out through deliverance.

ii.   Houses – Of course, a house can be demonized. Evil spirits can invade a house and make it uninhabitable for the owner or occupants. Have you not heard about houses that are haunted? I heard about a house in which a female shoe sound was often heard moving round the compound with a noisome sound. This was happening often within the later hours of the morning. That is mysterious indeed.

Again, in one of the schools in the eastern states, students reported that whenever they read late into the midnight, they often hear noises that looked as if soldiers were doing military parade. This was happening shortly after the war, when the spirits of the people (especially soldiers) were still parading. It was a Biafran military camp during the civil war.

In a particular instance, we were told that there was one that used to cry like a man forced to the war front, who never wanted to fight. And after some time, it would look as if he kept crying until he was killed unscripted. These are strange happening depicting demonic invasion.

I also heard about a case where closed doors were being opened by a strange force and this continued as a terror to the inhabitants. Indeed, there are haunted houses, and the spirits that haunt these houses terrorize the lives of the inhabitants.

iii.   Churches – Sure, a church can be invaded by demon spirit. How? A church which was used for prayer house practices with Cecelobia, gravel incense, angel-fill, etc., is already invaded by these spirits. Or do you not know that one bottle of Cecelobia contain many demon spirits? Indeed, a church such as this needs to be sorted out through deliverance.

On the other hand, if the vision bearer suddenly gets born again, adequate deliverance needs to be conducted on the place and on him. That is 'Operation-clear-the-area.' Otherwise, even if he wears the longest tie, the place and the person wearing the tie is already contaminated. This is so because he must have gone through a lot of demonic practices (both that of putting charms on the eyes and tongues), with which he was prophesying and seeing demons/spirits.

Some years ago, we went to a Church to minister to seven villages in the town. During the course of our prayer in the Church, a crocodile left the foundation of the church with tears pouring out from its eyes and cowries over all its body. When we tried to enquire from the priest in-charge of the church on what we saw, the man said that he was not the one that built the church. But he was told that the people who built this church had problem building the church. According to him, laying the foundation of the church was a tussle, as it was always falling each time it was laid. As a result, they went and called a marine priest, who lived not too far from the church. This marine priest used to call out mermaid (Mammy water), when he did, she would come and stand on the river while she talked and proffered solutions to people's problems.

However, this marine priest came and prayed (marine prayer of course) on the foundation and that was how the foundation of the church was laid. Do you not think that this church is a victim of demon spirits and that it needs deliverance?

iv.   Business – A business, whose foundation was built with the blood of cows or goat, is already contaminated. Such business is a victim of demonic spirit. If the owner suddenly gets born again, he needs to be sorted out. Also, the land needs to be redeemed from these demonic spirits.

v.   Human Beings – A person can be a victim of demonic spirit invasion. He/she can be contaminated by these spirits and needs to be sorted out properly. Until he/she is sorted out, living holy can be very difficult. It is when he/she is sorted out that he can now live holy.

This is when it will become very easy for him to walk in holiness. When holiness is achieved, then the third phase of Obadiah 1:17 come to bear - possessing his possession. Breakthroughs now begin to come.

Deliverance is the process and the effect of breaking the grip of evil family pattern over one's destiny.

Evil family pattern is very real. It plagues the lives of a lot of people. It can take the form of anger, immorality, awful occurrences in a certain period of the year, untimely death, strange accidents, poverty, late marriage, barrenness, unfruitful life, limitation, lying, profitless hard labour, etc.

Painfully, a lot of people come from a family with strong evil pattern and are labouring under the influence of such patterns. In such a family, for instance, anger (that traces down to the father) is like a tsunami. It seems to be running through their blood and manifests in the life of everybody in that family. In some cases, the explosion of this type of anger takes the form of the conglomeration of tsunami and hurricane. Now that you are born again, this evil anointing of anger must be broken. Otherwise, it is capable of denying you the Promised Land.

Recall that the anger, which existed in the tribe of Levi, limited the ministry of Moses. Moses was born with double-barrelled anger. The mother and the father were both Levites. Regretfully, he paid heavily for it because he ignored it and did not try to sort himself out. What you do not stop will stop you. What you hide is capable of disgracing you irrespective of the anointing in operation in your life. Be sorted out please. Moses' anger limited him. In the same way, the (unsorted) evil family pattern in our family can limit us.

There are others, whose evil pattern in their family is a curse – maybe the curse of immorality. I once counselled a man, who complained to me that his wife could hardly be satisfied with him. The wife lives immorally and wants to be allowed to just live her life. As the man studied the case, he discovered that the same anointing runs in the mother and also in the grandmother. Do they not need deliverance? Of course they need deliverance because this is satanic anointing, and if care is not taken care of, this kind of person is capable of tying a man to her will (with charms), so that she will be allowed to do what she wants. It is indeed complicating.

Hear me, before I was born, my family used to have accidents every March of a year, to the extent that even my father said that he does not want a March child in his house. It was such that every February, my mum would start writing us to remind us of March; a month that we were not supposed to travel to anywhere. But I refused to agree to this pattern when I noticed it was an evil pattern. We had to break that bondage, and too many good things now happen to me every March. It was prayer war, not just positive confession.

Deliverance is the process and the effect of liberating a person from the bondage of the forces of darkness – It guarantees freedom to a person who is bound by the forces of darkness and needs to be loosed like Jesus commanded: "Loose him and let him go." That is deliverance.

It is the release of a person, a family, or an organization from the bondage of strange happenings. Have you not heard about a person that has accident every two years at a certain period of the year? Do you not think that this person needs deliverance? Something is wrong somewhere. If that thing is not broken, it may consume him. He needs to be sorted out through deliverance.

Deliverance is the breaking of evil covenants and dedications that are holding people captive – Are you aware that some people were (erroneously) handed over to some spirits to either protect or look after them? In some cases, these dedications or covenants wreck the lives of such ones. To some others, these spirits dump them at crossroads of life, where it is impossible for them to make tangible headways, especially when they are not willing to keep to the terms of the covenant.

However, to get away from this grip, and be able to serve God truthfully, such people need to be taken away from such spirits. They need to be sorted out and be dedicated or covenanted to a Supreme Spirit, capable of guiding their lives jealously on a new covenant platform (the Cross of Calvary).

Some years ago, a very wonderful born again brother was having awful experiences. Unknown to him, his native doctor father consciously handed over the priesthood (to take over the idols) to him. But the father was alive when he got born again and he had told him that he would not serve the idols. The father smiled and said, "Do not mind." But, the idols were really dealing with him until he enquired.

Reading through the Bible, you will discover that God has given our parents authority over us. Recall that when God had covenant with Abraham, Levi and Jacob were not there? Their permissions or opinion were not sought for. But the covenant affected them. It is parental authority.

Again, when Israel refused to follow the covenant God made with Abraham, God whipped them. It is good you know, (especially the young ones) that this can never be addressed with "yee-men, leave this old man; they are of the Old Testament." Doing such is like digging your grave. Go and find out what your father has done on your behalf. Do something very fast, before you pay heavily for it. It could be your problem.

Also, I have a brother friend, who went to school and at the end was issued certificates. But, despite his certificates, he was going through problems that his certificates could not solve until we met. Firstly, while we were praying, God asked: "Are you now ready to serve Me?" And also asked us to tell him to go to his father and ask about the promise his father made concerning him. The young man went back to his father and the father shouted and said:

"I forgot to tell you that when you were born, you were very sick. And as my first son, you were taken to all hospitals without getting desired result. At a point, the doctors got tired, and everybody gave up hope that you would survive. I carried you to the altar of God and dumped you there. And said: God heal this boy and let him serve you."

He is a Canon now in the Anglican Church and a director in Civil Service. His life turned a new leaf when he began to serve God. That brother would have been wrecked if not for the step he took.

Beloved, make conscious effort to know what transpired over your life. Enquire the type of dedication that went over your life. Why? - If they did a negative dedication over you, it needs to be broken. It is not a one day prayer point. These things are spiritual matters, and some of them were conjured in layers. Some of them were done from altar to altar. Therefore, they require spiritual strategizing to be dismantled. Again, in-depth knowledge is a supreme factor for successful adventure is needed. Unfortunately, a lot of people do not have in-depth knowledge of spiritual warfare. As a result, they gamble into it and eventually complicate things.

In this type of dedication, you need to understand the nature of the things that were done by your forefather(s) and how they were done. Then, when you understand and know the level of what was done, you will be able to know how they passed it from the spirits of the land to the spirit in the heavens; how they visited the shrines and the altars to seal the dedication. How they handed it to the spirit of the market days, etc., so that sorting out will be very easy.

While you do this, bear in mind that light must conquer darkness. We are standing on the priesthood of our Lordship authority in Jesus' name, and we can cancel what the satanic priesthood has said. The one they said is rubbish.

Deliverance involves breaking demonic spells, and curses – Are you aware that what so many people who are sick today are suffering from is spells that have melted into their body? Once this spell is broken, he/she gets healed overnight.

A sister was sick. Her case was so bad and the doctors were managing her. As a result, she was living on drugs. We ministered healing to her. According to her, when she got home that day, she saw herself vomiting worms that filled almost a bucket in the spirit, and that was the end of the sickness permanently. However, if the spells were not broken, she would have possibly been going from hospital to hospital. The funny thing is that they were treating a spiritual matter with conventional methods. This brought complicated diagnosis.

Like I said, it takes a mystery to dissolve the mysterious. You do not solve a spiritual problem, by conventional means.

Deliverance is an authoritative release from the strongman that holds a person or a group of people captive – This is an authoritative move. As a matter of fact, there are some cases that we do not have to beg. You just have to tell the spirits that you are not negotiating with them. As a deliverance minister, there are times the demons tend to give some useless reasons for keeping their victim captive. Although, their claims or reasons might be very right if investigated, but then it is your duty to tell the demon that you are not negotiating – get out! But to do this, you need to be filled by the Holy Spirit.

There is a powerful man of God whose authority challenged me. He was a drunkard when God called him. This man followed God and began to drink the Holy Ghost the way he was drinking alcohol. They said if a demon case arises and other people were struggling and negotiating with the demonic spirit over the victim's deliverance, he would only walk down to the place and announce his name to the demons – "I am A.A Alien." The demon would run and the person would collapse. He did not even need to use the name of Jesus. That was a man who knew his authority in Christ. Are you that authoritative? Do you not see that authority is in levels?

Deliverance is the whole process; the result of breaking the claims of evil spirits over somebody – This goes to say that despite the claim of such spirits, you stand your ground and order them to move. You make them understand that he that is in Christ Jesus is a new creature; that the Bible says: "Whoever defiles the temple of God, God will destroy. This body is the temple of the Holy Spirit and because you have defiled it, we bring down the judgment of God upon you. Get out!" You have judged him and from that moment, his stay becomes very illegal.

Deliverance is the release from strange sicknesses and diseases –Sicknesses is a binding spirit. The breaking of that power is deliverance. Acts 10:38 says, "For how God anointed Jesus of Nazareth, who went about doing good, healing all that was oppressed by the devil." Most of the time, how he healed them was by casting out the spirit behind the sickness - and the deaf and dumb would begin to hear. It is deliverance!

Deliverance is the process of restoring a stolen star or destiny – Are you aware that some destinies or stars can be buried or stolen? Of course, some people's star have been stolen, covered, tapped into, vandalized, comfortably destroyed, etc. For some people, they need to fight to recover their star from where it was buried.

Sometime in the past, I was ministering to a brother, who was having quarrels with his brother. One day, the brother told him that they had discussion to make and asked him to come and pass the night with him. He agreed and they spent the night together. In the morning when they woke up, he discovered that he now stammers, while his brother (who was stammering before) was no more stammering. That is substitution – Demonic exchange. He came into our ministry and began to grow in the understanding of spiritual warfare. He went through deliverance and was restored while the stammering was returned to his brother.

Suddenly, he got married and to have children was a war because the brother was boasting that he would not have any child. Eventually, the wife became pregnant and later put to bed. The day his wife put to bed, he asked me whether he should tell his brother that his wife put to bed. I said, "Yes, since he is your elder brother." When his brother was told, he thanked God. But because he had conjured spirits to make the wife deliver through operation, he said: "Even though it was through operation." The brother then told him that the wife did not deliver through operation. He shouted in surprise and said: "The journey is still very far." As God would have it, he had other children.

Later, he decided to pack to another city. In that city, something else happened. According to him, God told him never to allow his children to enter into their neighbour's house. He called his house help, and told her never to take his children into the neighbour's house. The maid agreed. The day the devil came, their own television spoilt, and they were showing a very important television program. The house help ran into their neighbour's room and the children followed her. After watching the television, they went back. When he came back, nobody told him what happened.

By the next day, the neighbour's children protruded stomach became normal while his children's stomach was protruded. Thank God for that brother. He locked himself inside, closed his shop, fasted for three days, and commanded the protruded stomach back to sender; breaking the power that made it possible and destroying the projection. Within these three days, the children's stomach went flat and the neighbour's children stomach protruded again.

I want to encourage you my brethren, if you have not gone for deliverance, humble

yourself and go. It will do you a lot of good.
Much more than that, read good books on
deliverance.

CHAPTER TWO

SIGNS AND SYMPTOMS OF DEMONIC PRESENCE

I have discovered through personal experience in ministry that a lot of Christians are suffering in silence. Their spiritual pride is touched or punctured anytime you associate their experience with demons. I also discovered that a lot of Christians use demonic possession and oppression interchangeably, which is wrong. Firstly, I want to state that when a man is demonically possessed, it means that evil spirits have overtaken his spirits, soul, and body. The man is no more in control of himself but evil spirits now dictate his actions.

"And when he was come to the other side into the country of the Gergesenes, there met him two possessed with devils, coming out of the tombs, exceeding fierce, so that no man might pass by that way. And behold, they cried out saying, what have we to do with thee, Jesus, thou Son of God? Art thou come to hither or torment us before our time? (Matt. 8:28-29)

This is typical example of demonic possession. However, one is under demonic oppression when one or more evil spirits are squeezing him down, making life difficult and unbearable for the individual. They may even be afflicting him with sickness or misfortune, but the individual is mentally sound. He could be emotionally disoriented because of his sad experiences, but he is not mad. These spirits could be oppressing him from within and without or both. He is under demonic oppression or you can also say that he is demonized. This goes to say that some evil spirits have infiltrated his life. This can simply be connoted as demonic presence.

Believe you me, a lot of people are inhabited by evil spirits despite the fact that they are born again, speak in tongues, and come to church and fellowship. The question now is: Are there observable Signs and Symptoms that announce the possibility of demonic presence? How do you know that you are under demonic influence or oppression?

Here, we are going to look at behavioural patterns that depict whether an individual is under demonic oppression. They include:

1.　People That Hear Strange Voice

People who hear strange voices are under demonic oppression. The voices they are hearing are not the voice of the Holy Spirit, but the evil spirit. It also shows that spirits have a doorway into that life and sure needs proper deliverance prayer. For some, the spirits speak to them from outside through their ears. The spirits try to gain their obedience by telling them things that will happen before they happen. These are issues under their manipulations. If it is somebody they want to use as a native doctor or marine witch, they will be hearing the spirit or voice telling them that certain grasses or leaves cure this and that disease. In fact, while walking on the road, they will be hearing voices telling them the function of some leaves and barks of trees.

In some other cases, the spirits will be speaking from inside the heart. There are some cases where the spirits will be discussing immoral things that pollute the heart. Things the individual does not like, but he may not be able to stop them. This is common with ladies who were involved in water-based traditional dance like ejemiri, egedege, amala dance, owumiri dance, etc. At times, the spirits mock them, telling them, frustrating things and even encouraging them to commit suicide.

2.   Prevalence of Hereditary Sickness

Do you have a sickness that is hereditary? Probably, your mother had the sickness, your grandmother had it, and you also have it. Most of these sicknesses that run in the family line are demonic. They are caused by familiar spirits. A lot of them gained access into the family through sin. Thus, to deal with them, there is need to repent of the sins of the ancestors that opened the door for the spirits. Secondly, some of these hereditary sicknesses came because of family curses or even spells. Therefore, the curse or spell needs to be broken and the supervisory spirits behind them bound and cast out. It is strange to see a non-communicable disease being transferred from person to person along the family line. It can be from the mother line or through the father line.

3.   Nightmare Experiences

These are people who have terrible or dreadful dreams. A lot of them have sleepless nights while others are so eaten up with fear that they dread to close their eyes because of what they may see. These are demonic oppression experiences that need deliverance prayer to get rid of. A lady was always harassed and oppressed by python spirits in her dream. In one of her dreams, she saw herself in the midst of a large crowd as big as a market population.

In a twinkle of an eye, she heard an announcement of a man who said that he was looking for his wife. The whole crowd separated into two sides and she was at the centre. Suddenly, a python with a human head came and coiled around her. That was the beginning of a strange relationship with a very jealous spirit that never allowed any man to come close to her at all in any form. If she showed interest in any man, the spirit will appear and warn her never to try it. She was a captive of the mighty. A lot of people's faith has been thus destroyed by Satan. Some are so dominated that they are lured into satanic practices for solution. But, God has a promise for you:

"Shall the prey be taken from the mighty, or lawful captive delivered? But thus saith the Lord, Even the captives of the might shall be taken away, and the prey of the terrible shall be delivered: for I will contend with them that contendeth with thee, and I will feed them that oppress thee with their own flesh; and they shall be druken with their own blood, as with sweet wine: and all flesh shall know that I the Lord am the Saviour and thy Redeemer, the mighty One of Jacob (Isaiah 49:24-26).

4. Involvement in Strange Doctrines

False doctrines are the handiwork of seducing spirits. If anybody accepts or propagates a false doctrine, that person is under heavy demonic oppression. They are the works of evil spirits. There are different types of strange doctrines like:

i. Doctrines of the Pharisee (Math. 16:12).

ii.   Doctrines of man (Col. 2:22)

iii.   Doctrines of Devils (I Tim 4:1)

iv.   Diverse and strange doctrines (Heb. 13:9)

v.   Every wind of doctrine (Eph. 4:14)

vi.   Doctrine of Balaam (Rev.2:14)

vii.   Doctrine of the Nicolaitans (Rev. 2:15)

These strange doctrines are the handwork of seducing and deceiving spirits. Satan had a large well organized network. They are in groups or divisions set up to trap and enslave people through varying ways. In addition, they have done much for Satan in breaking the unity of the Church and Priesthood. They are also the sources of most blackmail which the whole Church shares. But the truth is that most of these doctrines are of no Churches at all.

5.   Compulsive Behaviour

There is demonic presence when a man has a compulsive behavioural pattern. This is a situation where somebody is compulsively or habitually tied to a behavioural pattern that he cannot even control. There are unseen forces compelling him to go ahead. It can be smoking, alcohol, drugs, etc., which he knows to be harmful, but yet he cannot stop it. He is not in control of his appetite. In most cases, demonic forces can be the propelling force to destroy his health and destiny. A lot of drug addicts do not like what they are doing. They know they have a problem. Some of them even cry about their problem, but it is a question of time, they are back into it. That shows there is a compulsive force (demons) propelling them to do what they are doing. To help people like these, there is need for personal discussion with the victim before and after deliverance prayers. You need to find out what led to the habit. The source of the problem will help greatly in healing him.

Funnily, a lot of people are addicts because of inferiority complex. Others are because of some sad experiences they had as a child. Imagine a child being beaten and told he was no good. "You are a failure: You will amount to nothing in life." "Foolish," etc. The child kept on hearing this same announcement each time the mother or father is annoyed with him. Later, some spirits will begin to help him believe that he is nobody and a failure. That breeds a complex. As he grows, you notice the child lacks boldness to do what his peers do. Now, he wants to be bold, and before you know it, he goes for drugs or "weeds" that will make him "high." That is how it starts.

6.   Occult Involvement

"There shall not be found among you any one that maketh his son or his daughter to pass through the fire, or that useth divination, or an observer of times, or an enchanter, or a witch, or a charmer, or a consulter with familiar spirits, or a wizard, or a necromancer. For all that do these things are an abomination unto the Lord – (Deut. 18:10-12)."

Occult involvement here includes witchcraft, magic, sorcery, necromancy, and trafficking of demon spirits. Thus, if you are currently involved in them, you need deliverance prayers. If you were once a member, but now you are no more practicing, you need thorough deliverance prayers to separate you from different spirits that have entered you through the initiation rites, oath of allegiances, oath of secrecy, positions held, spirits guides attached to you then, previous rituals and ceremonies, etc. You will need to be properly separated from their altars or you risk hindrances, nightmare, omens, or sickness the rest of your life, and in some cases premature death.

The minister will break your covenants with them and curse attached to you through the involvement. In fact, previous involvements of your parents in any of these practices are a satanic door for demonic oppression of your life. He could have dedicated you as a child. GO FOR PROPER DELIVERANCE PRAYER.

7.   Prevalence of Strange Sickness

Do you have a sickness you cannot understand? Are there sicknesses that go and come back again? Do you suffer from sickness that cannot be diagnosed medically? Is it a sickness that does not respond to medical treatment? It shows that evil spirits are at work.

There is no doubt that a lot of sicknesses are caused by evil spirits. During the earthly ministry of our Lord Jesus Christ, He healed the sick by casting out the evil spirits that caused the sickness. Today, it is not surprising to see a man sick and dying, and yet medical diagnosis reveals nothing. There are cases of strange movements in the body that defy healing. The live object moves round the body and finally comes back to take-off point. Both Ultra-sound and X-ray films cannot detect the sizable object, neither can the effect of its actions be medically defined. Yet, the victim is dying gradually. In such cases, the problem has a spiritual origin and Jesus is the answer. However, you need to cooperate with God.

8.   Suicidal Tendencies

"The thief cometh no but to steal, and kill and destroy (John 10:10a)

Satan is a destroyer and his agents have ways of propelling people to self-destruction. A normal human being will not wake up and decide to torture himself to death by hanging. He will count the cost, the pains, agony, and shame. However, under demonic influence, they do not remember their parents, wife, or children. These spirits fill them with an obsession to end their lives. A lot of suicidal tendencies start with hearing an inner or outer voice, even a compelling force telling them:

i.   **"Jump down from this building or height   and forget this world."**

ii.   **"Jump into this river and the troubles will   be all over."**

iii.   "Man die go (man will die). Run into the moving car and end these troubles," etc

Each of these cases is demonic oppression. They are under strong spiritual influence. An individual can also be so bewitched that he is used to destroy himself. I read a painful story of a woman who climbed a protective net and jumped into a breeding enclosure of more than twenty-five crocodiles. Naturally, they feasted on her. What a painful way to die. I do not believe that action was natural. The woman must have come under heavy demonic influence before she did that. Thus, every hidden or expressed desire to take one's life is a sign of demonic or evil influence.

9.   Deadly Poison

"The tongue is a fire, a world of iniquity, so is the tongue among our member, that it defileth the whole body, and setteth on fire the course of nature; and it is set on fire of hell. Every kind of beasts, and of birds, and of serpents, and of things in the sea, is tamed, and hath been tamed of mankind. But, the tongue can no man tame; it is an unruly evil, full of deadly poison: (James 3:6-8).

Scripturally, the tongue is very powerful. Word that rules the world is product of the tongue. It is because the tongue is a powerful instrument that Satan puts demons in people's tongues. Why? - Through such poisonous tongues, it is easy to destroy lives through the tongues of careless and thoughtless people. Therefore, if you have "diarrhoea of the tongue," you need deliverance prayers. If your tongue cannot be controlled, you are under demonic influence. If words coming out of your mouth are poisonous and injurious to the health of others, then it is more than ordinary. If words of your mouth pierce the hearts of others like deadly arrows, it shows that some spirits must have been attached to those tongues. Some people have lying spirits seated over their tongues. The result is that they tell lies anyhow. When you look at some of those lies, you cannot help but wonder why: What is the purpose of this lie?

10. Soliloquizing

This is the practice of talking to oneself aloud. They do not care if people are listening or not. The discussion is between oneself. He may be talking along the street, and yet talking to himself. This is a very demonic influence that can develop into mental illness, if not properly handled. In another case, the person talks to himself and at intervals, he laughs at times aloud. The person involved is under spiritual oppression, serious deliverance prayers are needed fast before the case gets out of hand.

11. Hallucination

Hallucination is a state of an individual seeing, hearing, or feeling what others do not see, hear, or feel. For those who are normal around, it sounds like imaginary things or fairly-tale. The fact of the matter is that they are seeing, hearing, or feeling spiritual beings.

Anybody who is seeing what others around do not see is under strong demonic oppression. In some cases, the spirits visit them, discuss or give them information while others are standing around without seeing the spirits. Sometimes, they flog them and torture them. You see them screaming in pain, but you cannot see those dealing with them. For others, the spirits appear to them and have given them the date they will die. People like these need our help. They are captives of the mighty.

12.   False Pregnancies

False pregnancy is a situation where an individual is having signs and symptoms of pregnancy, but she is not pregnant: Laboratory report shows she is not pregnant, ultra-sound says there is no baby in the womb, but her belly keeps protruding. She may even have other pregnancy signs. Most cases, the increase in the size of the womb gets to a level and stops. It remains like that for as long as twenty months or even more. These false pregnancies are hardly delivered while the people live in false hope. These are clear cases of demonic manipulations that have come to mock them. Most of these false pregnancies are caused by varying consultations for babies by people looking for the fruit of the womb. A lot of the people so visited by people with conception problem end up to be channels of demonic infiltration. There is need for caution and discernment. Do not be carried away by stories. A lot of the storytellers are satanic evangelists.

In addition, I want to state that some cases of barrenness are demonically induced and deliverance prayers are needed to clear the stumbling blocks and set the captive free. Experience has also revealed that evil spirits manipulate a lot of premature births.

13.   Strong Body or Mouth Odour

There are people that have very offensive body odour. For others, it is very bad mouth odour. No matter how much they bath, they still exude strong unnatural body odour. This is part of the reason people wear very strong perfume to cover their body odour.

However, I have seen that a lot of these cases change after long deliverance prayers. The body odour suddenly stopped. This shows that a very dirty, defiling/pollution spirit was resident in that life. You will remember that these foul spirits are dirty and come to pollute. Thus, they will not smell fine, otherwise, it will defeat the whole purpose.

14. Emotional Instability

Emotion has to do with the heart, thinking, feeling, and character. Every movement away from normal emotional behaviour is abnormal. A lot of emotional dislocations are manipulations of the negative spiritual influences of evil spirits. You are under demonic oppression if:

v   You are given to inherent jealousy of other people's success.

v   You are given to hatred, bias, and resentment.

v   You are given to hostility to people, easily angered, or given to wrath.

v   You are given to superiority complex (Self-idolatry), and inferiority complex.

v   You are given to nervous behaviours.

v   You have memory failure – many memory failures are as a result of demonic oppression. Some people cannot even remember what they read in the Bible before they finish two or three chapters. But when they read the newspaper, they remember the stories they read very clearly. That will show you the source of the problem. Demonic spirit is the source.

Some years ago, a man was brought to our ministry with memory failure. He could not remember what happened few hours behind, let alone the previous day. But when the spirits were cast out, he became normal again.

Another emotional problem is the spirit of segregation. It is an evil spirit. It destroys Christian unity. This is so called camp or party spirit. This spirit is more pronounced among the females. If somebody was under the influence and control of this emotional spirit, she chooses her friends from the group, or compound, or church. They have their own clique or group and that is where their love flows only. If you are not in the clique, you are in trouble. They have a visible or hidden complex or vacuum somewhere in their lives. Check such people, if they do not like you, if you do not meet their standard - that is if you are not accepted in their clique - even if you have a good talent or a good quality or you know the job very well, and they are in position to advance you, they will project someone else from their clique. It is not a spirit of Christ, but of the anti-Christ.

"Now I beseech you, brethren, mark them which cause divisions and offences contrary to the doctrine which ye have learned and avoid them – Rom. 6:7.

When ministering deliverance to people in this group, check out for subtle attachment of the spirit of sympathy and attention. This moves them to speak out for like minds that will service the spirit oppressing them with pity. They can include people with similar problems in their group, so that they can hold "pity party" together, once in a while. Probe for spirits of worry, jealousy, fear, and anxiety in their lives; it is hiding somewhere. May the Lord give us understanding.

15. Demonic Fears (Unnatural Fears)

The fear of the Lord is the beginning of knowledge (Prov. 1:7, 15:33). There is Godly fear and there are demonic fears. Fear is Satan's secret police. It is one powerful instrument Satan uses to destroy the faith of his victim and then keeps them in bondage. Satan uses fear to cause a lot of people to lose out of divine covering because he knows that the just shall live only by faith (Gal. 13:11), and that without faith, it is impossible to please God (Heb. 11:6).

Fear destroys your confidence in God and Satan is aware that whatever that is not done in faith is sin. That is why he hunts your life with fear to destroy your faith. Many people's fear has a long history. Some of them started as a result of previous but sad experience. Some are fearful today because of painful childhood memories. There are people who are so afraid that in the night, Satan whispers to them that they did not check under the bed and somebody could be hiding there. They will switch on the light again and again, checking and rechecking, showing the imaginations of enemies within. A lot of these people need healing deliverance prayers as spirits no doubt have penetrated them as a result of these fears.

There are people who are afraid of:

- Riding the motorcycle, no matter the situation.

- Height (even upstairs).
- Water, bridges, etc.
- Men/women.
- Marriage/marriage vow.
- Millipede (that does not kill)

16. Sexual Imbalance

There are a lot of sexual deviants. These are men/women whose sexual urges or practices are outside the accepted moral and social standards of godly societies. All such sexual imbalances are the works of filthy, defiling spirits. They are under demonic oppression or are downright Satanists out to mock God. They are propelled by fallen, rebellious spirits opposing the Word of God.

"Who changed the truth of God into a lie, and worshipped and served the creature rather than the Creator, who is blessed for ever Amen. For this cause God gave them up into vile affections: for even their women did change the natural use into which is against nature" (Rom. 1:15-26)

Today, sexual deviants are no more ashamed. However, let it be clear to you that they have an object of worship and that is Satan. In fact, sexual deviant behaviours are initiation rituals and sacrificial offerings at satanic cults. They say they conjure Satan in nakedness. It is heavy and deep. If you are or were involved, repent, confess your sins, and go for proper deliverance prayers.

i.   **Prostitution**

Prostitution is a demonic oppression. In fact, most of the prostitutes do not have any control over their sexual urges. When you talk to some of them, they shed tears, telling you that they do not like what they are doing, but the next day, they are back again. This shows that there are invisible forces compelling them to act that way. These are foul filthy spirits from hell. It is good you know that every prostitute is a witch. They are powerful instruments in the hands of Satan.

"Because of the multitude of the whoredoms of the wellfavoured harlot, the mistress of witchcrafts, that sellethnations through her whoredoms, and familiesthrough her witchcrafts. Behold, I am against thee, saith the Lord of hosts: and I will discover thy skirts upon thy face and I will shew nations thy nakedness, and the kingdom thy shame – (Nahum 3:4-5).

Prostitution is the grandmaster of so many vices and wickedness in the land. It is an evil wind that corrupts across lines.

"Do not prostitute thy daughter to cause her to be whore; lest the land fall to whoredom, and the land become full of wickedness." – Lev. 19:29

ii.   Exhibitionism

Exhibitionism is a psychosexual problem. There are people who like to exhibit their body (nakedness). They experience an inner sexual satisfaction by exposing their nakedness or the contours of their private parts. This evil spirit is rampant among ladies. Some adore their burst so much that they wear transparent dress without bra so that men or boys can admire them. It gives them great satisfaction. Today, these morally debased people are celebrated, and they have turned rich because of moral decadence.

The males who are possessed by these spirits love sleeveless T' Shirt and hot pants. A lot of them cannot wear their trousers on the waist but on the chest, thereby exposing the size of their male organs. Something is wrong somewhere. It gives them an inner sexual fulfilment, which many of them may not accept, but, they know it in their inner minds. Try to change them from the practice and you will find out it is a stronghold in their lives.

iii. Incest

This is the sexual relationship between a man and his sister. It is a sexual relationship between people with the same blood. It brings a curse. It opens the door to demonic oppression. I discovered that a lot of people are guilty and suffering today because of this error without knowing it.

Generally, a lot of them are not properly handled or were ignored while the victims labour under the curse or oppression without understanding the source of their problems. Firstly, incest is an abomination before God. Traditionally, it is an abomination in many cultures. Thus, even if you committed it when you were a child, you must address it because it could be affecting you now without your knowing it.

"And if a man shall take his sister, his father's daughter, or his mother's daughter, and see her nakedness, and she sees his nakedness: it is a wicked thing: and they shall be cut off in the sight of their people; he hath uncovered his sister's nakedness; he shall bear his iniquity." – Levi. 20:17

In every incestuous relationship, blood touches blood. Both incestuous relationships and marriage are demonically inspired. They are ancient practices of heathenish religions. The bottom line is Satan. Evil spirits follow such relationships. An evil sexual blood covenant is established. It can affect them psychologically. It can affect marriage in different ways.

iv.   Bestiality

"And if a man lie with a beast, he shall surely be put to death: and ye shall slay the beast. And if a woman approach unto any beast; and lie down there to, thou shall kill the woman, and the beast they shall surely be out to death; their blood shall be upon them." (Levi. 20:15, 16)

Despite the fact that we will no more kill the offenders because of the redemptive work of our Lord Jesus Christ, the fact is clear through the nature of the penalty that they are serious issues before the Lord. Bestiality involves sexual relationship between humans and animals. These abominations have been happening in real life. You will agree with me that it is totally strange and abnormal for man to enter into animals. That shows the level of demonic oppression on the individuals involved.

A man came to me and confessed his involvement in sexual relationship with a goat when he was a young boy. Today, he is married with children, a deacon in a Pentecostal church, but he cannot control his sexual urges. When the spirits came over him, and the wife was not around, even in the night, he would move out and rape somebody. It could be a girl lying outside in search of flesh air or one that left the door open to let in air. Facially, the spirits affected his image badly. His problems were many. Satan is wicked.

v.   Lesbianism

This is sexual attachment or relationship between a female and another female. It is highly demonic. If you are involved in it or were involved in it, you need deliverance.

I have ministered to a lady who told me that Satan gave her some power to go and destroy the world. When I cross-examined her on the issues, she confessed that she had some evil powers that affect mainly the females. "What is this power?" I demanded. She said that any time she comes into the company of other females; they will begin to hunger sexually for one another. Firstly, that shows that lesbianism is demonically motivated. It also shows that human agents or initiates of this Satanists' cult can manipulate and lure others into it. It attracts serious curses like homosexuality. In fact, lesbianism is female homosexuality.

"If a man also lie with mankind, as he lieth with a woman, both of them have committed an abomination; they shall surely be put to death; their blood shall be upon they." – Levi. 20:13

vi.   Homosexuality

Homosexuality is sexual attachment or relationship between a man and another man. It is an anti-Christ spirit that opposes accepted Biblical principles.

"Thou shall not lie with mankind, as with womankind: It is abomination." – (Lev. 18:22)

Homosexuals are deviant personalities. Today, they have strong, organized membership cults mobilizing weak souls for Satan. You cannot be involved in homosexuality without demonic infiltration. It is common among Satanists, and it attracts curses from God of heaven and earth.

A lot of rich men with satanic wealth are involved in homosexuality. Painfully, they have penetrated the ranks and files of the churches. These are abnormal behaviours inspired by fallen spirits. Otherwise, what is a normal human being looking for in the anus of his fellow men? All kinds of veneral diseases are rampant among them, chief among which is HIV/AIDS. No wonder the Bible says:

"And likewise also the men, leaving the natural use of the woman, burned in their lust one towards another, men with men working that which is unseemly and receiving in themselves that recompense of their error which was meet. And even as they did not like to retain God in their knowledge, God gave them over to a reprobate mind, to do those things which are not convenient." – Rom. 1:127-28

vii.   Seductive Force

Do you have seductive force? It shows that there is oppressive spirits working through you. If as a man, you discover that women are seriously charmed by your presence or find it difficult to refuse your immoral overtures, then you need spiritual help.

However, if you are a woman, and once men see you, they are mesmerized; they may not know why, but they feel seriously enticed to have you, there is a spiritual problem. You may be a good Christian, even the man may be. But once men see you, their hearts are undressed out of righteousness. You have heavy seductive spirits. These spirits can make a Bank Manager go into a housemaid without knowing what came over him.

OTHER SHADES OF SEXUAL IMBALANCE INCLUDE:

- Fornication and Adultery
- Voyeurism
- Masturbation
- Rape and sadism
- Transvestism
- Porno-films (pictures/magazines, films, etc.)

17.   Compulsive Stealing

Some of them steal things they do not even need, or things cheaper than the ones they have.

18.   Constant Accidents

19.   Disappearance of things. - It could be money.

20.   You come into a new place you have never been to physically, but the whole environment looks familiar. It seems as if you have been there before.

These issues are all signs of demonic presence. The list if not comprehensive enough, will nevertheless open your eyes. It will also help direct your prayers. The issues raised require violent deliverance prayers, and you will be free.

CHAPTER THREE

LAWFUL CAPTIVE

Some people say careless things, which sound good to the ear, but the truth is that they are not applicable. Sometimes, you hear words like: "What I do not know, does not know me." – Lie! What you do not know can know you even more. For example, some people are in prison for an offence they never knew when and where it was committed. In US, a man was already put on an electric machine to be stemmed for a murder he did not commit.

Unfortunately, the man who committed the murder covered it beyond discovery and ran away. But the mother of the man who was held captive came to the altar of God and begged the man of God to pray. In her words, she said: "In the next fifteen minutes my son would die for an offence he did not commit." For the cry of the mother, the pastor prayed. Suddenly, they (executioners) had a phone call three minutes to the time. The executioner picked the call and the caller said: "Do not kill that man. He is not responsible for the offence. I am the one who did it."The executioner asked; "Who are you? Who are you? Where are you? The caller replied: "I am some few mitres away. I am coming. Do not ask me any more questions. I am coming down to give myself."

That stirred up confusion among the executioners. Upon that confusion, they decided to wait. After a while, the man came. They interrogated him and said: "This case had gone through a lot of trials and there was no where your name was mentioned. What made you decide to open up now? The man said: "I do not know. A force came upon me and I could not just help but confess. I am the man who committed the offence."

This picture is a self-explanatory indication that what you do not know, can know you, and not only knowing you, it can keep you bound throughout life if nothing is done. In other words, it can make you lawfully bound or a captive for a lifetime.

Painfully, a lot of people are moving in chains, even though they seemingly appear free. One can be trapped consciously or unconsciously. But, whether you know it or not, captivity is as real as life and death. Shockingly, some are under the captivity of the mighty for self-implicated reasons amidst other reasons. Thus, they are lawful captives.

WHAT IS LAWFUL CAPTIVITY?

Lawful captives are those that transgressed or offended or are guilty. Put in another way, a lawful captive is a person that is under captivity because of his/her offense, share-offence or inherited offence. The enemy thus has right to attack him/her.

Lawful captivity is a real and Biblical fact. God Almighty knew that man at one point in life, can become a prey (lawfully) in the hand of the mighty. Hence, He promised deliverance. Talking about lawful captives, the Bible says:

Isaiah 49:24-26

"Shall the prey be taken from the mighty, or the lawful captive delivered? But thus saith the LORD, Even the captives of the mighty shall be taken away, and the prey of the terrible shall be delivered: for I will contend with him that contendeth with thee, and I will save thy children. And I will feed them that oppress thee with their own flesh; and they shall be drunken with their own blood, as with sweet wine: and all flesh shall know that I the LORD am thy Saviour and thy Redeemer, the mighty One of Jacob."

"In meekness instructing those that oppose themselves; if God peradventure will give them repentance to the acknowledging of the truth; And that they may recover themselves out of the snare of the devil, who are taken captive by him at his will." II Tim 2:25-26

WHO IS A LAWFUL CAPTIVE?

1.   EVERY UNBELIEVER -

Anybody who is not born-again is a lawful captive because he/she is not in the kingdom of God but in Devils'. Satan has every right over them and can experiment any kind of sickness he has on them. Recall that the Bible says: "The day you gave your life to Christ, you are translated from kingdom of darkness into the kingdom of light." Thus, there is change in position -THAT IS THE BIBLE! It does not matter what you think or what your pastor says.

2.   CHRISTIANS THAT LIVE IN SIN –

Know ye not, that to whom ye yield yourselves servants to obey, his servants ye are to whom ye obey; whether of sin unto death, or of obedience unto righteousness? But God be thanked, that ye were the servants of sin, but ye have obeyed from the heart that form of doctrine which was delivered you."

Rom. 6:16-17

If you are a Christian and still lives in sin, Satan has right to take hold of you. I listened to a tape about a girl. She was going mad. The family carried her to a pastor. The pastor began to command the spirit to go. While he commanded, the spirit spoke and said: "What is your business in this matter?" The man of God said: "You must come out." The spirit replied: "Okay, I will leave, but this girl is very immoral. Our agent/member has his seed inside her. When she leaves here, she will still go back to commit another immorality with him. And if she did that, we will have her killed before she is brought back to you."

Also, I read in a book, a confession by an occult grandmaster on how he killed a minister of God. He said that he wanted to kill this minister, but it was difficult for him. At first, he released four hundred demons to follow the man. Later on, one of the demons came and told him that about sixty-seven demons of lust had invaded him. On receiving the information, he released the spirit of death to follow the minister. He did this so that the spirit of death could attack him any day he committed immorality. The occult man said that it really took time to get even with the minister, because he struggled with the immorality. One day, he committed immorality and that was the end of the minister's life. Now, when we gather to bury the minister, will anybody know what happened at the last minutes of his life? Let him that thinks he stands, take heed lest he falls.

3.   CHRISTIANS THAT DISOBEY THE CALL OF GOD

"Now the word of the LORD came unto Jonah the son of Amittai, saying, Arise, go to Nineveh, that great city, and cry against it; for their wickedness is come up before me. But Jonah rose up to flee unto Tarshish from the presence of the LORD, and went down to Joppa; and he found a ship going to Tarshish: so he paid the fare thereof, and went down into it, to go with them unto Tarshish from the presence of the LORD. But the LORD sent out a great wind into the sea, and there was a mighty tempest in the sea, so that the ship was like to be broken. So they took up Jonah, and cast him forth into the sea: and the sea ceased from her raging. Then the men feared the LORD exceedingly, and offered a sacrifice unto the LORD, and made vows. Now the LORD had prepared a great fish to swallow up Jonah. And Jonah was in the belly of the fish three days and three nights."

Jonah 1:1-4; 15-17.

The scripture above showed that Jonah ended up in the belly of a fish because of disobedience to the call of God. In the same way, the problem of some people is that they are too busy to give God time. Unfortunately, when you are too busy to give God your time, God will allow your enemies to keep you busy and probably make you their captive. I always tell people that whoever finds it difficult to serve God will serve his enemies and Satan – (Combined Honours)! You must create time for God. He is a jealous God. If you want His covering, you must give Him your time. He does not like being used as a spare tyre, and that is what most of us make of Him. When we are finished in our jobs and tired, (even when our dresses are rejecting us), that is when we run into fellowship. Even while in the fellowship, some will be busy with their phones. Each time I see people pick phone calls in the church, I know that I have seen people who have a disdain for God and spiritual order.

Hear this: Christians who do not have time for God will soon become lawful captives. When the devil comes after them, God will be too busy to spare His own time for them.

There was a story about a sister who was always living carelessly, despite the warning of the man of God. One day, the minister told her that the day she will be attacked, God will be far. Unfortunately, the day they attacked her (a nurse, but a Christian), it was at night. They targeted the day that the Evangelist (who is their leader in the hospital and whom they fear) was on a night off. The day they hit her, they were the same people that came with string to inject her. But she told them not give her any injection, but to take her to the Evangelist's house. Shockingly, the person that attacked her was her closest friend. How was that known? The man of God prayed and she died, but refused to confess.

4. CHRISTIANS THAT EAT THEIR SEED

"While the earth remaineth, seedtime and harvest, and cold and heat, and summer and winter, and day and night shall not cease." - Genesis 8:22

5. CHRISTIANS THAT REFUSE TO PAY THEIR TITHES

"Behold, I will send my messenger, and he shall prepare the way before me: and the Lord, whom ye seek, shall suddenly come to his temple, even the messenger of the covenant, whom ye delight in: behold, he shall come, saith the LORD of hosts. But who may abide the day of his coming? and who shall stand when he appeareth? for he is like a refiner's fire, and like fullers' soap: And he shall sit as a refiner and purifier of silver: and he shall purify the sons of Levi, and purge them as gold and silver, that they may offer unto the LORD an offering in righteousness. Then shall the offering of Judah and Jerusalem be pleasant unto the LORD, as in the days of old, and as in former years. And I will come near to you to judgment; and I will be a swift witness against the sorcerers, and against the adulterers, and against false swearers, and against those that oppress the hireling in his wages, the widow, and the fatherless, and that turn aside the stranger from his right, and fear not me, saith the LORD of hosts. For I am the LORD, I change not; therefore ye sons of Jacob are not consumed. Even from the days of your fathers ye are gone away from mine ordinances, and have not kept them. Return unto me, and I will return unto you, saith the LORD of hosts. But ye said, Wherein shall we return? Will a man rob God? Yet ye have robbed me. But ye say, Wherein have we robbed thee? In tithes and offerings. Ye are cursed with a curse: for ye have robbed me, even this whole nation. Bring ye all the tithes into the storehouse, that there may be meat in mine house, and prove me now herewith, saith the LORD of hosts, if I will not open you the windows of heaven, and pour you out a blessing, that there shall not be room enough to receive it. And I will rebuke the devourer for your sakes, and he shall not destroy the fruits of your ground; neither shall your vine cast her fruit before the time in the field, saith the LORD of hosts. And all nations shall call you blessed: for ye shall be a delightsome land, saith the LORD of hosts. Your words have been stout against me, saith the LORD. Yet ye say, What have we spoken so much against thee? Ye have said, It is vain to serve God: and what profit is it that we have kept his ordinance, and that we have walked mournfully before the LORD of hosts? And now we call the proud happy; yea, they that work wickedness are set up; yea, they that tempt God are even delivered. Then they that feared the LORD spake often one to another: and the LORD hearkened, and heard it, and a book of remembrance was written before him for them that feared the LORD, and that thought upon his name. And they shall be mine, saith the LORD of hosts, in that day when I make up my jewels; and I will spare them, as a man spareth his own son that serveth him. Then shall ye return, and discern between the righteous and the wicked, between him that serveth God and him that serveth him not."

Malachi 3:1-18.

Christians who refuse to return their tithes are thieves. The Bible says: they have two charges.

6.   CHRISTIANS THAT TAKE GOD FOR GRANTED –

What do I mean? These set of Christians have a way of clashing with authority. When you come into the house of God, know that God has His own spiritual authority. The man of God may not have a certificate; better keep your own certificate. That is a spiritual house, not an academic environment.

Today, a lot of people (even professors) are having problems because they had problems with a pastor, who is a West African Examination Council Certificate (WAEC) holder and does not even speak good English. It has ruined and wrecked a lot of intelligent brethren, who would have been useful to God.

Beloved, when you get to a spiritual house, behave yourself.

Recall:

KORAH'S INCIDENT

Numbers 6:1-

SON'S OF AARON

Leviticus 10:1-; I Sam 13:8-14

They were Levites. He came from the tribe that was supposed to produce the priesthood. All of them were leaders. The Bible calls them "Elders of the people." They were not even ordinary, but they crossed their boundary. The day Moses prayed, heaven responded and did the unusual (see: Numbers 16).

So, even as an elder/deacon in the church, you must know that God has hierarchy. Do not cross your boundary. People who over-step their boundaries become lawful captives. For instance, we were in a church (Pentecostal church), whose pastor had three cars. In that church, there were other two brothers who had cars, but theirs were not very much okay. So, some of them were jealous. They were not happy. Meanwhile, God called the pastor at the age of seven and he answered God. He did not go to school, but he was useful to God. This church that he pastored was filled with lecturers and well educated people. It was as if God surrounded him with that calibre of people.

One day, there was a clash. The youth got offended with this man. When the youth found out that some of the elders were biased about the man, they filed up charges against him. One of the days, they removed the pulpit and protested that he would not preach until he rendered account. Hear this: All of them have not recovered from that incident, except one girl. She was advised to go and beg him (the pastor). She was told to insist on his forgiveness and prayer, even if he insults or pushes her out. She was the only one that was humble to do that, and was the only one that got married out of all the girls. Beloved, when you see a spiritual authority, be careful!

7. THOSE WHO HAVE GIVEN THE ENEMY THEIR SOUL BY COVENANT –

Those who wilfully gave themselves to Satan are lawful captives.

8. THOSE WHOSE FATHERS ATE IN SATAN'S HOTEL

"The curse of the LORD is in the house of the wicked: but he blesseth the habitation of the just." – Proverb 3:33

Those with wicked pasts have their results in the future, waiting.

9. GUILTY AS CHARGED –

Example, a person who had finished serving his master, but still sees himself serving the same man and the wife. Why will you not you serve him? You know that the man is not a Christian and has some errand spirits working for him, yet you were busy stealing his money.

By this act, you have fallen prey into the hands of his altar and the spirits working for him. He then tied you there – that is a lawful captive.

May I say this, so many people are passing through series of awful experiences because of what they did or where they went. When I was in one of the secondary schools, I had a student who was the class prefect and the most intelligent. But nobody knew that the boy steals. One of the days, his class members contributed money for condolence, but he stole it and said that it was missing. The students came and called me. When I got there, I opened Zechariah 5 – "The Mystery of the Flying Rope". After reading it, I told them that the person who stole the money should bring it out. I also told them that if the person refused, I was going to tell the angel of Zechariah 5 to come after the person. I went further to say that if after reading the scripture and nobody brought out the money, we would all go. After reading the Bible, nobody brought out the money even till the next day. I came the next day and read the scripture and released the angel called "the flying rope" against the person that stole the money.

Talking about this angel, the Bible says that it goes to the house of the thief and stays there until he concludes the job for which he was sent.

Unfortunately, as at six years after his secondary school (by the time I saw him) he had not been able to pass his WEAC exams. You know it can be frustrating, when an intelligent student misses admission for six years. His life and personality will be affected by the experience.

Have you tried to find out whether you are responsible for what is happening to you?

As at now, men are looking for the virginity of the girl they will collect to service their altar. Painfully, many of the girls do not know. I listened to the cassette of a boy. This boy said that he had used thirty-seven wombs of women to service the spells he used in boosting his business in Onitsha, until Jesus caught him. Funny enough, these girls come for deliverance prayers, and never tell us how it happened. They are lawful captives. As a girl, if the man that deflowered you was a native doctor (and many were deflowered by a native doctor), prayer house prophet, occult man, Muslim, or an Asian, you are a lawful captive. In fact, you need serious deliverance. As a matter of experience, if I tell you what many girls had gone through because of careless and loose life, you may not help but shout.

One day, while we were conducting deliverance for one of the girls, God said that we should pray over her private parts. Taking heed, I asked one of my daughters to lay her hands on her while I laid my hands on that my daughter, and I said: "Lift up your heads o ye gate and be ye lifted up, ye everlasting doors." While we prayed, men were driving out from her private parts. When we were through, I did not understand the revelation. But my daughter whom I prayed with began to ask her questions on the men and the cars, which she saw driving out from her private parts. As she questioned her, the girl started crying. That was an undergraduate of Law. But you know she walks around normally and did not know she had a complicated case.

These are lawful captives. It may interest you to know that this does not affect only women/ladies. It also affects men/boys. I have on my iPad, story of a girl who told me that the problem she is having now is the boy she deflowered. She is a cult girl. She deflowered this guy to rekindle her powers. Now, the boy has gotten born-again and is going through deliverance sessions. As a result of the fire coming from him, she gets tormented even while walking on the road. As a result, she is looking for a way to be released from the trouble. May I add that some people find it difficult to pray the prayer of deliverance, because what is keeping them bond does not want them to be set free. Secondly, they do not want to come out of their problem. Thus, they cooperate with them because they do not know that somebody is making a gain (financial/spiritual) out of their bondage.

How do you reconcile this? A girl came to our ministry and while we prayed for her, the Lord said: "Look at her breast."There were two human eyes on her breast, in addition to her own human eyes. I asked the Lord for the meaning. The Lord said: "Ask her where she went." She said that she was taken to a river by a native doctor at night. After bathing her in the river, the native doctor had sex with her there. That stands to say that he had sex with her in his altar (river), because the man is connected to the river by covenant. Again, by that act, the man has planted his spiritual seed into her.

Note: Every sexual relationship is a blood covenant, an exchange of seeds, a soul-tie, spiritual marriage, etc.

By the time that girl left, she never knew that as she was walking around, she was a living sacrifice. The human being who had eyes inside her was drawing power from her and was adding it to his own. In that case, he had duplicated his power and that had made him a powerful native doctor. The girl does not know that she is now a mobile altar of the man.

Consequently, every other man entering into her is already having spiritual complications. WHY? The native doctor is collecting his power from him through his intercourse with his mobile altar – the girl he slept with. LIKE I SAID, THESE ARE LAWFUL CAPTIVES.

10.   IGNORANCE –

The Bible says: "They know not, neither will they understand, they walk on in darkness" (Psalm 82:5). Painfully, there are people who do not know and do not want to understand. The result is that they remain captives. There are some deliverances that come by knowledge. Recall that the Bible says:

"And ye shall know the truth, and the truth shall make you free" – John 8:32.

"Wisdom is profitable; in all you get, get wisdom and understanding – that is knowledge" Proverbs 4:5.

Knowledge comes from reading and learning from others, who had made it. Through personal devotion, commitment, and eagerness to embrace knowledge, liberation comes. For instance, as you read this, there are some changes that are taking place in your spirit man. These changes are what galvanize your deliverance, and they are made possible through information gathered from this piece. May I repeat that so many are dying because they do not know, and do not want to understand. People perish for lack of knowledge. Knowledge is power, knowledge has power. Do all you can to get knowledge; never joke with knowledge.

Today, a lot of people are in captivity and are dying because they do not want to get knowledge. I do not joke with knowledge. Sometimes, I sleep very late at night reading books. You need to study books and find out what is happening around your life; you need information.

Quite uninterestingly, some of us sit down for hours watching films, but will not give time to reading the Bible or books. The world is ruled by ideas. If you must rule your world, you need ideas and information. The problem we have is lack of knowledge and information. Information is power; those who value it, invest in it.

11. SEPARATING WHAT GOD HAS JOINED TOGETHER IN MARRIAGE:

Recall that the Bible says: "What God has joined together, let no man put asunder" (Matthew 19:6). I know a case of a woman who was married into a family. This woman was being maltreated by the husband and his sisters. They would call for family meeting and ask the woman to leave. When the woman tried to protest, they told her that she was too wise.

One of the days, she said to the husband's sisters: "But for one of you who would marry, and who must see what I saw here, all others must stay back to marry your brother with me." As at now, her children are already in secondary school. Not one of them married except that one, whom she said would marry, and for that one that married, the husband beats her mercilessly. When there is a spiritual law, do not break it.

The Bible says: "Do not treat treacherously, the wife of your youth" (Mal. 2:15). It is a commandment. This means that when you deal with her treacherously, you break a spiritual law and must go into spiritual prison. As it is in the physical, so it is in the spiritual. When you break a physical law, you go into physical prison. When you break a spiritual law, you go into spiritual prison. SUCH PEOPLE ARE LAWFUL CAPTIVES.

12.   BORN AGAIN CHRISTIANS THAT ARE LIVING IN UNFORGIVENESS:

"For if ye forgive men their trespasses, your heavenly Father will also forgive you: But if ye forgive not men their trespasses, neither will your Father forgive your trespasses." – Matthew 6:14-15

If you have decided to walk in unforgiveness, you are a lawful captive. Nothing hinders healing like unforgiveness. The Bible says; "The anger of a man can never work out the righteousness of God" (James 1:20).

13.   ANGER AND PRIDE

"Ye have heard that it was said by them of old time, Thou shalt not kill; and whosoever shall kill shall be in danger of the judgment: But I say unto you, That whosoever is angry with his brother without a cause shall be in danger of the judgment: and whosoever shall say to his brother, Raca, shall be in danger of the council: but whosoever shall say, Thou fool, shall be in danger of hell fire. Therefore if thou bring thy gift to the altar, and there rememberest that thy brother hath ought against thee; Leave there thy gift before the altar, and go thy way; first be reconciled to thy brother, and then come and offer thy gift. Agree with thine adversary quickly, whiles thou art in the way with him; lest at any time the adversary deliver thee to the judge, and the judge deliver thee to the officer, and thou be cast into prison. Verily I say unto thee, Thou shalt by no means come out thence, till thou hast paid the uttermost farthing." – Matthew 5:21-26.

14.   BITTERNESS

"Follow peace with all men, and holiness, without which no man shall see the Lord: Looking diligently lest any man fail of the grace of God; lest any root of bitterness springing up trouble you, and thereby many be defiled" – Hebrews 12:14-15

15.   INGRATITUDE –

Ingratitude is the worst of all vices and even God hates it. Some people remember people and their relations when they have problem. When the problem is solved, they tend to forget and do not have "Thank You" in their mouths for those who helped them while they were down with problems. The Bible says: "Whatever you sow, that shall you reap" (Gal. 6:7). You must learn to appreciate people who God has used to bless you in life. Learn to appreciate people God uses to cross you over in life. They do not owe you anything. They had their own problems, yet they helped you. You must learn to appreciate and be a blessing to them. It is a bad spirit which I have seen in this part of the world. Our people are very ungrateful.

16.   BORN AGAIN CHRISTIANS LIVING WORLDLY

"Whosoever therefore shall break one of these least commandments, and shall teach men so, he shall be called the least in the kingdom of heaven: but whosoever shall do and teach them, the same shall be called great in the kingdom of heaven." – Matthew 5:19

CHAPTER FOUR

EVIL COVENANTS

PART I

A lot of people are suffering because of the evil covenants they got involved in knowingly or unknowingly. Some of such people have frustrations, while some will tell you that they are having strange accidents, mysterious sicknesses, madness etc. Worse still, some of them feel like committing suicide. To some others would write an exam, but their papers will not be found.

Can you imagine that a person sat for JAMB exams, had better score necessary for admission, applied to one of the universities for higher studies, and was supposed to study a regular course there; after the admission process, he was not offered admission. Rather, his form was discovered in another university, quite distant from the university where he applied, to study a course education, which he did not tender any application for? How do you explain this? One of the perfect explanations to this mysterious experience can be traced down to evil covenants.

Evil covenants operate with spirits who witnessed the covenant process and who have the charge/assignment to supervise the articles of the covenant. These spirits can do things. They hardly forget, because they are very focused on the assignment. Although we can forget the covenant and its articles as humans, these spirits do not forget.

SORRY STORY

I read a story in one of the books written by one of the powerful deliverance ministers respected all over the world. In his book, he talked about a girl, who would sit for an exam that comprised of nine papers, in which there is paper one, two, and three. At the end of the exams, her papers would not be found. Although it would show that she sat for the exams, and that she submitted her papers, not one script would be found. This happened three times - that is three wasted years, before she could realize the source of her problem.

What happened?

There was a boy she had blood covenant with and they promised to marry themselves. Eventually, the marriage did not push through. In the end, that covenant was what was ruining her. It was when it dealt with her up to three times, that she now confessed. Funnily, she was going for deliverance for three years, and never revealed this within these three years. This is the case with some people who keep some of the truths or facts about their lives that will help in their deliverance.

It is quite worrisome that many of us who come for deliverance are not sincere or honest enough with God. They withhold the vital information. Of course, the devil will be smiling because they have protected him. The Bible says that he that covers his sins shall never prosper: but whoso confesses and forsakes them shall have mercy - Proverbs 28:13. When you confess your sins, you will find mercy.

Indeed, evil covenants wreck lives and limit great destinies, especially when not addressed properly. It affects marriages, and is one of the great factors behind barrenness, marriage problems, no direction in life, even poverty and untimely death.

In the light of this, the question that comes to mind is: how are these covenants cut/entered into or contacted?

These covenants can be contacted through:

a. River-bathing

b. Saraka

c. House cleaning (i.e. family deliverance with false prophets). This is capable of bringing more demons than the one brought by the shrines and idols that were there before.

d. Intake of mustard seed in the name of deliverance.

e. The use of the blood of goat to cleanse the land. Recall that the Bible says that blood defiles the land. This brings complications. Be careful with the person you bring into your house to pray. You must study his history. Know who made him and the spirit he is carrying. Otherwise, he can get you into more problems.

f. The use of candles for prayer – In the book of 3 John, the Bible warns that you should not encourage them. If they come without this gospel, do not encourage them.

g.   Purchasing or reading magazines of false religion - You do not have the backing of heaven to buy some of the magazines of false religion. False religions are sponsored by spirits, and you cannot keep them in your house without being affected by these spirits.

Do you not know that having yoga or some of the cult books in your house can make you vulnerable to evil spirits' penetration? How many of such books are in your house? You better go and cleanse the house.

I remember one of our wonderful sisters, who was very zealous to serve God after giving her life to Christ. Although she had cleared her house of everything that she knew that honoured Satan, there was still resistance. One day, she said she had a vision and saw herself in her library. There was a spirit wearing black on black. When she asked the spirit what he was doing there and tried casting him out, the spirit replied saying: "Here is my home." The spirit refused to be cast out, and she was almost losing her voice before she woke up. By the breaking of the morning, she was at my door to ask for the meaning. I told her that there was a property of Satan in that house. She said: "It is not possible." Then, I reminded her that the spirit said it was his home. There were accursed materials in her house. I asked her to go back and go through the books one after the other. As she did that, she discovered one yoga book, which she bought many years ago in London. That was all. We prayed and destroyed it and that oppression stopped.

DIVERSE TYPES OF COVENANTS

1. **Generational Covenants**— This came because our forefathers served some idols, which made them to enter into some covenants. Funny enough, many of us today are aware that our parents served idols, but we choose to deceive ourselves. Amazingly, because some of our fathers knew what it takes

to bury a heathen, they may wake up one morning when they are about to die and decide to join a church. But that does not cancel the fact that while he was a heathen he had some unbroken covenants, which is capable of wrecking the whole family if not addressed. There was a particular girl who got mad eventually because of such covenants. Recall that you were in his loins when he was making sacrifices to these idols. Tell me why it will not affect you if you do not go to be sorted out properly. Do you not know that you need to be sorted out?

In Scriptures, Abraham entered into a covenant at the time he had not had his first child. According to the Bible, he paid tithe to Melchizedek. What is the Bible saying? Abraham had a covenant with the priest of God, Melchizedek – first generation man. When he entered into this covenant, Isaac was not yet born. He paid tithe to him and they ate together. Invariably, this covenant was entered by tithe paying and eating together. When Isaac was born, he transferred the covenant to him. When Isaac had Jacob, he transferred same to him that is the third generation of Abraham.

In the fourth generation, Jacob had twelve sons, and one of them was Levi. The Bible says that this Levi paid tithe also. How? He was in the loins of Abraham, when he paid tithe to Melchizedek; and when he paid tithe, Levi paid tithe. Levi was also covenanted from fourth generation (Gen. 14:17-20; Heb. 7:1-10).

However, when your own father and forefathers were at their diverse idols, you were in their loins. When they were celebrating idols and sharing meals at these idol stations, you were in their loins. This is why deliverance is important. I have seen a lot of Christians and ministers suffer because of these covenants, simply because they do not want to pay attention to it.

Many years ago, when we started teaching on deliverance, it was not very popular. Hence, there were a lot of people who did not believe in deliverance, and the teaching of deliverance was not very rampant. Within that time, I invited a man who was a bishop and asked him to speak about Unity of the Church in our conference. Instead of preaching about unity, he took time to dismantle my deliverance ministry and me while talking to my audience. I sat down and was looking at him. When he finished, I collected the microphone from him and did not say anything about what he said. After the meeting, a young man called me and told me that he had a message for the bishop that preached.

According to him, when the bishop was preaching, the Lord showed him an idol in the bishop's father's compound that was knocking everything the man was doing down. He went further to say that this man was supposed to be a great man of God, but his ministry is suffering. WHY? An idol in his father's compound was dealing seriously with him. He begged me to relate these messages to him, but I refused and told him to go and tell him since he was the one that received the vision. How could I who invited him to talk about unity, only to witness him dismantling deliverance, talk to him about such a thing?

In less than one year, that idol reduced the bishop so much so that his sitting room became the headquarters of his church. Today he is ashamed to answer bishop. He now answers apostle.

A lot of Christians are suffering in silence. Some of them are quoting stories which they hear the white man quote that they have not experimented.

2.   **Dream Covenant** —You can enter into an evil covenant through your dream. Pathetically, a lot of strange happenings in the lives of many people are as a result of the dream they had, which they took for granted. Again, lots of people have entered into marriage covenant with strange beings through their dreams, and the result is that they keep having repeated experience of sexual intercourse with this strange being each time (or often) they close their eyes to sleep. Many

have also entered into witchcraft and secret cults through their dream.

There was a brother who is a minister now, but formerly a member of a secret cult. We led him through renunciation prayers while we were conducting deliverance for him. But after his renunciations, God said that it was remaining Freemasonry. When we asked him about it, he said that there was never a time he joined Freemasonry. When we told him what God said, he became quiet for a while. After some time, he said that he was told in the dream that he is now initiated into Freemasonry some years back.

The question is: How many have been initiated into witchcraft through their dreams, with or without knowing? How many have been initiated into the water cult through their dreams?

Some years ago, I remember a case about a daughter of one of our church leaders. While we were ministering deliverance to her, the Lord said that she was initiated the previous night. Amazingly, the revelation was a confronting one because deliverance was not popular then. As a result of the revelation, the girl and her sisters were angry to such point that they almost pulled down the whole fellowship. They had felt that the integrity of their family was at stake. At the other end, I was also in trouble because it was not a popular thing.

However, while everybody was in that confusion, I asked her whether she wants to see how she was initiated and she said "Yes." So, I told her to close her eyes and I asked God to open her eyes to show her the initiation ceremony. After some time, she began to shout, "No, No, No." That 'shouting' gave me boldness to shun her and ask her to shut-up. Since she could not shout when the initiation was carried out, and could not talk when the sisters almost pulled down the fellowship, it was too late to shout.

3.   **Evil Covenants Through Sexual Relationships** – Sex outside marriage is very evil, illegal, and can mar great destinies. One act of

sexual immorality outside marriage can destroy your destiny. Sex is life; it is the giving out of life. It is a blood covenant. It is an exchange of seeds. It brings a soul-tie covenant.

A lot of things such as spirits, demons, personal evil covenants, evil dedications, family and personal curses, blood, and organisms are exchanged through sexual intercourse. Even gifts are transferred. In the light of this, picture what happens when a man or woman commits immorality with a Muslim or native doctor. Recall that their allegiance is to another god. So are the spirits and covenants they are involved in.

However, it may interest you to know that any man or woman, who has had any immoral relationship with a Muslim, should consider him/herself a person that needs to be sorted out via deliverance. And he/she needs to start with a proper repentance prayer to God. Why? He/she has allowed a Satanist to mock God. How? When he was coming into her, he was coming to conquer the person and her

God, and God was watching when this was happening.

Again, imagine people who had slept with a native doctor. How many spirits and covenants do you think were exchanged by that act? Worse still, many had this sexual intercourse with the native doctor in front of his shrine, when they were taken to the river for river-bathing. Astonishingly, when such people come for deliverance and are asked to fast, they will start arguing. Even when they start the deliverance, they will not finish it. They treat it with so much contempt and care-free attitude.

Think about what it looks like when one has sexual intercourse with a prayer house prophet, particularly those with Dread-locks. Such a person has gotten a complicated initiation. Do you not think that there are no people who have such complications? Of course there are. Unfortunately, some of them did not know where their destiny got lost. But I am here to tell you that was the day trouble entered. Supposed it was a Hindu or a cult boy;

how about those who have been used by animals? The Bible says it is confusion.

4.   **Religious Covenant** – There are religious covenants. Your past and present involvement in false religion ties you into a religious covenant, and until that covenant is broken, something is wrong. It can hinder your life. It can even be the reason you have not been baptized in the Holy Ghost.

I met a woman in my early years in ministry, who came from one of the greatest churches in the nation. According to her, she had been prayed for severally by heavily anointed ministers, yet she found it difficult to receive the baptism of the Holy Spirit. This confession almost discouraged me from praying for her. But somehow I gathered courage to pray for her. Before I started praying, I asked her whether she had gone to any prayer house before now. She vehemently said "YES." That was what hindered her from receiving the baptism of the Holy Spirit. Why? She was being prayed for without being sorted out through deliverance. Worse still, she did not reveal that aspect and the ministry where she worshipped did not believe in deliverance.

Having known this, I then asked her to go and do proper renunciation prayer. I gave her the prayer guide and she went to do so. On the last day, she came. While we worshipped God (before we knew what was happening), she started blasting in tongues. Do you see the difference?

For many years, you cannot cast out headache because you are still a religious man. The fact that you can quote forty or fifty scriptures offhand does not make you a spiritual man. That is the problem some of us do not know. Many of us are just religious men claiming to be spiritual men. But I encourage you to be spiritual.

5. **Idolatrous and Heathenic Covenants** – Looking at the name idolatrous and heathenic covenants, they depict evil covenants, one contacted through heathenic and idolatrous practices. You may be in the

Church, yet by practices and involvements, you can get into some of these covenants. Some years ago, one of the sisters in our fellowship said she embarked on prayer, asking God what is in her life that offends Him. God opened her eyes and showed her a revelation that traced back to her days in primary school as a young girl, with dress tied round her breast, while she danced a traditional dance. God asked her what they were singing then. It may interest you to know that some of these traditional songs, praise mermaids and Satan. Funnily, those who sing them do not know that they are blasphemous words. Pathetically, they have brought some of these songs into the church and nicknamed it – Church song.

You may not know the problems that are involved when one gets into traditional dance, especially those songs that are in honour of Satan or his cohorts. I have been a deliverance minister for close to thirty years and I can tell better. I have seen lives ruined because of covenants that they never took seriously – things they thought did not matter.

I had a colleague whose husband was well to do. One of the days, she walked into my office for counselling, but could not talk because of profuse flow of tears. This is a beautiful wealthy woman, and the husband takes care of her. After sometime of encouragement, she opened up to me. According to her, she said that most of her husband's friends, who come to the house in the name of looking for her husband, were actually coming for her. Again, everywhere she went to, men would turn once they set their eyes on her and would be making advances at her. Yet this is a married woman with children. Worrisomely, as a result of this experience, she came to ask whether there was anything wrong with her.

In response to her question I said 'yes', because there is a strange spirit inside you. You are carrying a strange seductive spirit. If you discover that when men see you they get mesmerized and undressed, there is a strange seductive spirit following you.

On hearing this, she then asked me how it could have come. I gave her a lot of instances and asked her whether she was involved in traditional dance. She said 'YES'. She was the LEAD singer, who used to carry the serpent. I conducted deliverance on her. But that was one deliverance I will not forget in a hurry. The deliverance took quite some time. While it was on, I had so much trouble than imagined. Spirits were rioting against me and were manifesting wickedness through human beings. It was indeed a horrible experience.

Do you have such problem? Do men get mesmerized when they see you?

Listen, it is not only women that are caught in this web; men are also affected. A man can have such spirits. Are you aware that there are men that once women set their eyes on them, they will feel like going to bed with them? Men like this have such seductive spirits that can keep a woman's head spinning. It can also make a woman lose so much control over her womanhood, irrespective of how much a taboo it is in our society. If you are such a man, you need deliverance.

Do you know that there are twin rituals, marriage rituals, new-yam festival rituals, chieftaincy title rituals and the like? All these can be a means of contacting idolatrous or heathenic covenant.

Again, shaving of hair when somebody dies leads somebody into a heathenic covenant, because those covenants are coming from darkness, and the Bible says that you should not shave your hair for the dead. These are how different demonic covenants are entered into.

6.   **Occult Covenants** – A lot of us were not there, but our relations were there. If you entered into occult before or presently, you were into an evil covenant. From the time you began to fill their form through the initiation rituals to the regular membership sacrifices, different levels of covenants are contracted. In addition, you swore a lot of oaths such as oath

of allegiance, oath of secrecy, oath that you will be a permanent member, etc. Remember that these oaths are taken before the shrine and idols, and that the priest administers a blood covenant alongside such oath-taking. Curses are pronounced in case anyone breaks the covenant.

If you have been involved in the occult, please go for proper renunciation. When you go for deliverance, please be honest. You need to reveal all that you were meant to go through, while your initiation ceremony was conducted. Why? If you begin to hide some things necessary for your deliverance from this group, you will have problems. In a bid to hide some things while renouncing involvement in occult, many have experienced strange sicknesses and even death.

This is same with the AMORC. At a stage in their initiation, the person being initiated will see himself go through a door that is closed, before he enters their celestial sanctum. Now, you are born again, if you are not delivered from that gate, your body will be stupidly looming in the church while your spirit is caged somewhere. That is why you see many of them, especially some of the strange ministers, who know that God did not call them in the area of deliverance, mismanage the situation. The result is that we lose many of them. Some of them have strokes, and other sicknesses.

I remember one particular case, which a young man shared with us. They managed and prayed some funny prayers and burnt the documents without sorting the man out through deliverance. Suddenly, his car that was packed in the garage, started itself, and after spinning for some time, the car went into reverse and came out of the garage and stopped. In the morning, the man had stroke. These are spirits and they came through covenants. If God did not call you into deliverance please do not handle such, so that you do not cause more problems.

Unfortunately, it is only in the church that every pastor claims to know everything. It is good you know that one sees in the spirit does not mean that he can handle everything. Some matters are handled by calling. Every calling has a provision. In the hospital, you will see doctors who are Dentists, and you cannot refer a pregnant woman to them. Neither can you refer a person having a dental problem to a Gynaecologist. But that is what happens in the church, because most of our pastors are not enlightened, or are ruled by pride. Please I like to advise that a Paediatrician should not say that a Dentist is not important. They are all doctors. Until you suffer from severe tooth ache, you will not know that tooth ache is worse than surgical cases.

Brethren, there is nobody God has given everything. When somebody claims to have everything, arrogance has come, and that spirit is from hell. Calling and messages are not the same. When a preacher begins to teach, you will discover that he struggles and finally gambles into error if he is not an old established minister. Therefore, we should be able to correct some error, before the church goes wild.

Still on occult covenant, you can enter into the occult covenants through reading their books. This is why you should avoid those books. You can enter by reading about your star on newspaper. Visiting their agents in the name of checking what your star holds through your palm. Please do not show any man your palm. Anybody who wants to see your palm is not from God. I do not care the size of Bible he is carrying or has on his pulpit.

Are you aware that there are occult flowers? There are occult flowers, and they are heavily demonic. Keeping them in your house can covenant you.

Sometime in the past, I went to the house of a man for deliverance prayers. This man was very learned, and he studied overseas. When we were done and were going home, he showed me a flower, which he asked whether we should destroy. I was a young man in ministry then, so I told him not to, unless they are demonized. When he asked further, I explained to him what I learnt from my Japanese and Korean arts. I told him that there is a religion in Japan which involves the keeping of flowers. The man smiled and said: as long as this flower is here, even if armed robbers move round this building and come back, they will never knock on this door. I then said that the flower is demonically sophisticated more than the police barracks and needs to be destroyed. Is that a simple flower? NO! You can also learn more about this if you go to enquire on this from a horticulturist, who is a Christian. Are you aware that some of them hear the voices of the flowers? Again, you also discover that some of the cult groups' headquarters look like a flower garden.

7. **Evil Soul-Tie Covenants** – A Soul-tie is an invisible thread that seems to link, bind, or yoke one man to another. There are good soul-ties. For instance, there is a good soul-tie

between my wife and I. The result is that we may be at different locations, thinking about similar things at the same time (Deut. 10:20; I Sam 18:1).

Know also that there are evil soul-ties. This occurs when there is an ungodly yoking together between two souls in an unholy alliance. It can open any of them to demonic manipulations. It can come because of past sex life or the practice of lesbianism or homosexualism between the two. It can come as a result of an oath or vow of secrecy between two people. It can come because of broken marriage vows, and evil spirits can use it to plunder and wreck lives.

Can you picture how the soul-tie between Samson and Delilah manipulated the life of Samson - even at the risk of his life? Samson knew very well that this girl wanted to destroy him, yet he walked into the plot that destroyed him. Today, there are girls like that. A man would beat the hell out of their head and instead of separating from the man for a while, they would still stay and die in the name that they love him - Stupidity first class! The truth is that there is a demonic soul-tie.

There was a girl who was in our ministry that nearly went mad. Unknowingly, there was a soul-tie between her former boyfriend and her. This former boyfriend was a wizard without her knowing. This wizard gave her a photograph during one of the valentine seasons. In that photograph, the guy opened two holes in the pictures, representing the both of them, before giving her the picture.

What did they give you as valentine gift? Only God knows what happens between 13 and 14 February of every year.

In the case of this girl, the boy released spirits into the picture that he gave the girl. Viewing the picture spiritually, you could see demonic spirits looming round it. When this girl got born again, she did not deal with the manipulations on the photograph, and the result was that whenever she started praying in her room, it would look as if a hand was spinning her head round. We had to go there, prayed, and discovered what was in the picture. Funnily, destroying the photograph was like breaking her heart. But because she was almost going mad, she had to give up. There was also cassette that the boy gave her. This cassette is where every radio and music she used to listen to were being transmitted from.

On seeing all this, I made her to understand that there was a serious soul-tie between the boy and her. As a result, it had such manipulative force that could make her abandon everything she was doing to go and meet him, whenever he called. She agreed and confessed that the boy was like her small god and whenever he called her, she would rush to answer him.

Unfortunately, some people do not know what is going on in their lives. Therefore, I want to advise that when you are asked to pray, you better pray, so that your destiny can change for good. You have managed enough. You have

been scratching and scratching, and that cannot
be the plan of God for your life.

CHAPTER FIVE

CURSES AND RELEASE

A curse is an evil pronouncement intended to afflict, harass, oppress, or destroy the victim. The victim of a curse can be a person, family or property. It is an invisible force you cannot see with the naked eyes, but the reality of its opposition or havoc is unmistakable.

A curse can also mean the roadblock or blockade that stands between you and success in life. It keeps a life limited and distant from breakthroughs. Call it a supersonic dark cloud covering a person's or family's star from shining; it is not far from that.

A curse can also be defined as the supernatural words of evil, energized by God or Satan with the ability to wreak havoc or destroy destinies or personalities.

Curses are a supernatural force that influences or opposes people's lives or property for evil. They are evil words or negative sentences packaged to injure or destroy living or non-living things. As a destiny destroyer, curses prevent a person or family's destiny from full manifestation.

"And Noah awoke from his wine, and knew what his younger son had done unto him. And he said, cursed be Canaan: a servant of servants shall he be unto his brethren. And he said, blessed be the Lord God of Shem: and Canaan shall be his servant God shall enlarge Japheth and he shall dwell in the tents of Shem; and Canaan shall be his servant

(Gen. 9:24-27).

Today, a lot of destinies have been limited, frustrated, and some destroyed because of curses. So many people are labouring under varying degrees of curses. There are individual, family, village, town, estate, and national curses.

Curses bring a covering of darkness and as a result, hinder the light of development, success, and even educational attainment. Notice that in towns and communities that are labouring under the curse of idolatry and bloodshed, nothing moves there. They may be popular for producing powerful native doctors, but no development. In fact, they are rather famous for producing house-helps, unskilled labourers/workers, and wickedness. Their children are fetchers of water and hewers of wood. It is a curse.

Curses are more extensively widespread than we have ever imagined. Virtually all areas of creation can be cursed. Take for instance, land, farm, business, family, children, health, animals, estate, town, and even a country can be cursed. A Church or the minister could be labouring under a curse. A lot of Christians are labouring under varying degrees of curses. A lot of health problems, fertility and financial calamities are visible manifestations of curses.

Curses have ruined a lot of lives because of ignorance (Hosea 4:6).

"My people are destroyed for lack of knowledge. Because you have rejected knowledge, I also will reject you from being priest for Me."

Unfortunately, the Church/minsters are not teaching this, and those who do are so cautious or diplomatic that they do not state the hard facts. Take for example, some people claim that a Christian cannot be cursed. I do not want to argue about that but what type of Christian? Is it the Christian that sows discord or divides the Church of our Lord Jesus Christ without the fear of God? Is it the one that castigates and even preaches another servant of God from his pulpit? Is it the 419 Christian? It is the pastors that will use their fellow pastors to gather and bless his people and at the end, send him home without something to buy bread for his family? All these cases and more bring curses, and a lot of Christians and ministers are suffering from it (Rom. 16:17-18; Gal. 6:7-8).

"As the bird by wondering, as the swallow by flying, so the curse causeless shall not come" – (Prov. 26:2)

There must a cause before a cause can stick. One truth we must face is that the type of Christianity that we practice today is lacking in humility, integrity, and brokenness. This inglorious Christian lifestyle provides a lot of openings for curses to penetrate. Today, a lot of professing Christians do not show the difference between the clean and unclean (Ezek. 22:26). What we have in abundance are men and women who are full of head knowledge of the Word of God, but whose hearts are empty of God. That is why there are too many so-called wisdom preachers that cannot cast out headache. The word and the

Spirit is the power of God, but these people are lacking in the Spirit. They lack the covering of the Spirit, but are full of physical violence. The Holy Spirit cannot live in them.

Also he sent forth a dove from him, to see if the water, were abated from off the face of the ground. But the dove found no rest for the sole of her foot, and she retuned unto him into the ark, for the waters were on the face of the whole earth: then he put forth his hand, and took her, and pulled her in unto him into the ark (Gen. 8:8-9).

This is a story we are all familiar with. After the flood, the earth was still covered with water when Noah decided to send out the dove to survey the land. Unfortunately, the dove could not find dry land for the feet to rest, so the dove returned to the ark. Sincerely, this is the sorry picture of some Christians today. After lots and lots of revival meetings, the dove of heaven descends, but there are no prepared heart altars for the Spirit to tabernacle. Our hearts are dry of love, empty of compassion, joy, peace, kindness, patience, self-control, and gentleness that are the enabling environment for the Holy Spirit to operate.

Believe me, lives that are full of pride, anger, envy, competition, lusts, wrath, jealousy, covetousness, political manipulation, etc., are open to the curse of the enemy. Why? There must be a doorway for a curse to enter. There is always a reason for a curse to stick.

"He that diggeth a pit shall fall into it; and whoso breakethan hedge a serpent shall bite him (Eccl. 10:4).

The principles of God demand that exercise out liberty with utmost wisdom. Thus, if you move out of the boundaries of divine law and protection, the enemy can hurt you. God has some natural covering over all His creation. This covering ensures that the wolves do not eat-up all the sheep (I Sam. 17:43). He knows there is a thief here that he has come to steal, to kill, and to destroy.

However, whosoever breaks these coverings, Satan or his cohorts can bite him.

Why? There are divine laws and principles sustaining these coverings and once they are violated, the enemy is given a doorway for a legitimate attack. This fact is made clearer by King Solomon:

"As the bird by wandering, as the swallow by flying, so the curse causeless shall not come (Prov. 26:2)

Curses cannot stick on you unless there is a reason. That is why Balaam said: "Surely there is no enchantment against Jacob, neither is there any divination against Israel" (Num. 23:23a).

I have often seen and heard believers quoting this scripture. But sometimes, I discovered that the people using it have never taken time to digest the whole affairs. Why was Balaam not given permission to curse but to bless? The answer is in verse twenty-one (Vs. 21):

"He (God) hath not beheld iniquity in Jacob, neither hath He seen perverseness in

Israel; the Lord is with him, and the shout of a king is among them (Num. 23:21).

This is part of the reasons I insist that a lot of Christians are working under curses without knowing it. God saw no sin in Jacob and insisted that Balaam will not pronounce his curses. Remember that those curses were energized by seven demonic altars and power flows from the altars. If they were ordinary words, God would not have made all the efforts to stop him. He knows better. Remember, the words of Jesus:

"For the prince of this world cometh, and hath nothing in me" (John 14:30b).

If Satan comes and finds some of his properties in you, he can use them to steal your joy. Thus, if the divine principles ensuring your supernatural covering from God are respected and obeyed, a new curse cannot penetrate your life and affairs. However, if there was a curse on your life before, you will do well by addressing it properly. The reason is because a curse will continue to flow until it is broken. A life of holiness can weaken the manifestation of an already existing curse, but surely sin fertilizes curses.

SOURCES OF CURSES

There are different routes through which a curse can come or enter to afflict lives.

1.   Curses can come from God (Gen. 3:17-19; Gen. 12:1-3; Gen. 27:29; Deut. 27:15-26; Ps. 16:4).

2.   Curses can come from an angel of God (Judges 5:23; Luke 1:19, 20).

3.   A minister of God can be the source of a curse (Josh. 6:26; II Kings 5:27; II Sam. 1:21; Acts 13:11; II Tim. 4:14).

4.   Generational curses exist: These curses are mostly inherited and come because of where you were born (Gen. 49:7 – i.e. Solomon and Levi. This also hindered Moses from entering the Promised Land. Num. 20:8-12; Ex. 20:5; Prov. 3:33).

5.   A lot of people are suffering because of curses they pronounced upon

themselves. They are called self-imposed curses (Gen. 27:13; Num. 14:1-3; Matt. 27:24-25).

6. Curses can come from satanic priests (Num. 22:24; I Sam. 17:43).

7. Parents can curse their children, consciously or unconsciously (Gen. 9:25; Gen. 49:3-7; Eph. 6:1-3).

8. Environmental curses exists, and people living in such places can be affected without knowing it (Judges 5:23; II Sam. 1:21; Matt. 11:21).

9. A husband can curse the wife and the wife can curse the husband (Eph. 5:21-24; Gen. 31:32; Mal. 2:13-16).

OTHER SOURCES OF CURSES

1. Refusing to come to the Lord's help (Judges 5:23).

2. Doing the work of God deceitfully (Jer. 49:10; Mal. 2:6-17).

3.   Keeping accursed materials in your house (Deut. 7:25-26; Ezek. 44:23; Acts 19:19).

4.   Failing to give glory to God (Mal. 2:1-7).

5.   Involvement in false religion (Jer. 44:7-8; II Cor. 11:13-15).

6.   Sexual perversion (Rom. 1:25-28; I Cor. 5:1-5).

7.   Stealing God's tithes and offerings (Mal. 3:8-11; I Cor. 9:6-7; Hag. 1:2-11).

8.   False prophets are cursed (Deut. 18:20-22; Deut. 13:1-5).

9.   Children who curse their parents bring a curse upon themselves (Ex. 21:15, 17; Prov. 39:17; Heb. 10:26).

10.   Covenants breaking – Breaking vows or agreement attracts a curse (Josh. 9:15-19; II Sam. 21:1-6). This includes marriage vows.

11.   Putting your confidence in man instead of the Lord (Jer. 17:5).

12.   Causing anyone for whom Christ did to stumble in faith (Matt. 18:6-7; Deut. 13:6-10).

13.   Teaching the Israel of God (Christians) rebellion against God or His statutes (Jer. 28:15-16; Deut. 13:5; Num. 16:1-50).

14.   Abortion brings curses (Ex. 21:22-23).

15.   Belief in stars (Horoscopes) (Jer. 10:2-5; Deut. 4:19, 26-27; Deut. 17:2-7).

16.   Failing to rebuke sinners of their sins (Ezek. 3:18-21; Rom. 1:32).

17.   Rewarding evil for good brings serious curses (Prov. 17:13; Ps. 109:4-20; Jer. 18:19-23).

18.   The curse of the Lord is upon homosexuals and lesbians (Rom. 1:26-28).

19.   Shifting landmarks (Prov. 22:28; Rom. 23:10, 11).

20.   The curse of the Lord is upon the thieves (Zech. 5:1-4; Prov. 28:20).

21.   Adding and subtracting from the Word of God brings a curse (Deut. 27:18-19; Deut. 4:2; Prov. 30:6).

22.   Do not use foul language against leaders of God's people, church elders, authorities, including Satan. It can expose you to a curse. E.g. "Satan is an idiot," is not scripturally permitted to curse him despite the fact we must NOT honour him (Judges 8-11; II Peter 2:11-13).

23.   Sponsoring false religion, buying their literature or sacrificing to strange spirits brings curses (II John 9:11; Deut. 17:2-6).

SIGNS AND SYMPTOMS OF CURSES

Below are simple and common signs or signals of the manifestation of curses in a person's or family's life.

1.   Fruitless hard labour/struggles.

2.   A cycle of evil repayment.

3.   Delayed marriage or marriage problems of varying degrees.

4.   Compulsive   alcoholic consumption or smoking.

5.   Chronic servitude. You can never be in charge but tail always.

6.   Reproductive   problems   e.g. barrenness, miscarriages, impotence, low sperm count, etc.

7.   A cycle of premature death of the male population.

8.   All female birth without male (e.g. six to seven female children without a male child).

9.   Outright poverty or persistent hindrances or financial insufficiency.

10.   Mental   illness   or   generational madness.

11.   Immorality as a family sin e.g. the parents are immoral and the children are likewise.

12.   Multiple problems - There is always something to mourn about.

13.   Hereditary diseases that are not even communicable e.g. bronchitis, high blood pressure, diabetes, asthma, etc.

14.   Always a victim of one form of accident or the other.

15.   Unwarranted suspension and removal from office - Take for instance, some people hardly stay long on a job without a problem.

16.   Chronic foundation layers - When the work begins to blossom, they will be transferred where they have to start again: "Original suffer-head."

17.   Strange deformities and retardations from birth are as a result of curses.

18.   Strange victimizations - It is like people derive pleasure in maltreating you.

FREEDOM FROM CURSES (KEYS TO FOLLOW)

1.   Take time to discern and identify the prevalence of curses.

a)   This can be by simple observation.

b)   Ask God to show you the source of your problem, with prayer and fasting.

c)   Discuss with your parents, grandparents, and/or elders of your family.

d)   Study your family history and pay attention to re-occurring experiences.

2.   Absolute determination to be free is very important. You must be ready to pay the price needed for your freedom (Fasting, prayers, mid-night watches etc).

3.   Repentance from every personal and family sin that opened you up for the curses.

4.   Repent of all hidden biases against God and accept God's forgiveness for you. It is wrong for you not to forgive yourself after God had forgiven you. Forgive all those you are holding in unforgiveness. Remember, God will forgive you according to the measure you are able to forgive others. Without sincere

forgiveness, you cannot be forgiven (Luke 6:38).

5. Renounce all strange covenants, dedications, charms, and initiations in your life.

Ø Renounce all agreement your parents and grandparents have with demon spirits.

6. Use the power that is in the Name of Jesus and break every curse that is oppressing your life. Destroy the effects and control of such curses in your life and destiny.

7. Clear your house and environment of all accursed materials and destroy them (spiritually and physically).

8. Deal with the spirits behind the curses (supervisory spirits).

9. Prophetically pray for restoration of all that the enemy had stolen. Pray for divine blessings.

10. Stop speaking evil of yourself and situation. Be positive (Job 3:25; Prov. 18:21).

PRAYER FOR FREEDOM

1.　　Take authority over every curse that might be working against you as a result of negative words released against you.

2.　　Pray and destroy every self-imposed curse you might have brought upon yourself or destiny.

3.　　Repent and pray to release yourself from every curse that is working against you for breaking human or divine vows.

4.　　Pray and command every curse that is working against you for partaking in foods sacrificed to idols or demon spirits to be broken.

5.　　Command charms and representations working against your life to be destroyed by fire.

6.　　Revoke all evil decrees, decisions, and judgments passed against you in the physical and in the spiritual realms.

7. Take time to break every curse of evil repayment, limitation, hindrances and poverty working against your life.

8. Speak into all the rooms in your house and command fire to locate and destroy all demonized items, gifts, etc., in the house.

9. Repent and use the blood of Jesus to revoke and destroy every curse brought upon you by your parents, guardians, school teachers, or boss.

10. Revoke and reverse every curse of destruction handing over your life.

11. Bind every spirit supervising a curse against your life.

12. Pray and destroy all invocations, incantations, and spells working against your life.

PRAYER POINTS

DELIVERANCE PRAYERS

Scriptural Verses: Gal. 3:13-14; Col. 2:14-15; Luke 10:19; Rev. 12:11

1.   I renounce and destroy all hidden covenants with demonic powers, in the Name of Jesus.

2.   I renounce and destroy all evil parental soul ties, in the Name of Jesus.

3.   Whatever the Lord has not planted in my life, be uprooted by fire, in the Name of Jesus.

4.   By the Blood of Jesus, I break every family and personal curses working against me, in the Name of Jesus.

5.   In the name of Jesus, by the blood of Jesus, I separate myself from the collective captive of my family.

6.   I renounce and destroy all inherited demonic covenants, in the Name of Jesus.

7.   I renounce and bind every family strongman oppressing my life, in the Name of Jesus.

8. I renounce and destroy evil dedications working against my life, in the Name of Jesus.

9. I renounce and destroy every covenant with idol spirits, in the Name of Jesus.

10. I renounce and destroy all demonic initiations, in the Name of Jesus.

11. I bind and cast out all demonic spirits oppressing my life, in the Name of Jesus.

12. I renounce and destroy the controlling power of evil altars, in the Name of Jesus.

13. I renounce and destroy every witchcraft covenant and initiation, in the Name of Jesus.

14. I renounce and destroy all demonic marriage covenants, in the Name of Jesus.

15. I break the controlling powers of spirit husband/wife over my life and affairs, in the Name of Jesus.

16.   I renounce and cast out of my life, the spirit of reincarnation, in the Name of Jesus.

17.   I renounce and destroy every covenant with the python spirit, in the Name of Jesus.

18.   I release a heavy artillery bombardment of destructive fire against spiritual forces contrary to my life and destiny, in the Name of Jesus.

19.   I renounce and destroy all ancestral covenants and bondages speaking against my life, in the Name of Jesus.

20.   I renounce and destroy all ancestral dedications, in the Name of Jesus.

21.   In the name of Jesus, by the blood of Jesus, I reject and destroy every promise of service made to strange spirits by me or for me, in the Name of Jesus.

22.   I renounce and destroy every covenant with water spirits and water goddess, in the Name of Jesus.

23. I renounce and destroy all 'Ogbanje' and 'Uke' covenants speaking in my life, in the Name of Jesus.

24. I revoke and destroy all sealed and unsealed covenants with the water spirits, in Name of Jesus.

25. I severe every communication and cooperation between my spirit and dark spirits, in the Name of Jesus.

26. I speak into the waters; visible and invisible waters; and I command all my held blessings, star, marriage, breakthrough, certificates, organs, etc., to jam fire, in the Name of Jesus.

27. Every marine agent, manipulating my life, jam fire and die, in the Name of Jesus.

28. Let the controlling powers and influences of my foundational idols/altar over my life be destroyed by fire, in the Name of Jesus.

29. I renounce and destroy the controlling powers of the ancient family charms over my life, in the Name of Jesus.

30.   I bind and terminate the assignment of strange spirits from my family trailing my life, in the Name of Jesus.

31.   I renounce and destroy by fire, every blood covenant with Satan through incisions/marks, in the Name of Jesus.

32.   I renounce and destroy every strange covenant with Satan through the burial of my umbilical cord, in the Name of Jesus.

33.   I renounce and destroy by fire, all sacrifices, libations, and rituals to demonic spirits, either by me or for me, in the Name of Jesus.

34.   I renounce and break every soul-tie covenant between me and any man/woman, dead or alive, in the Name of Jesus.

35.   I renounce and destroy by fire, any involvement with:

v   Secret cult

v   Witchcraft cult

v   Occult

v   Water cult, in Name of Jesus.

36.   I renounce the meetings and initiations of every secret cult, in the Name of Jesus.

37.   I renounce and destroy the altars and property of any secret cult linking me, in the Name of Jesus.

38.   I withdraw my spirit, soul, and body from the controlling influence and power of any secret cult, in the Name of Jesus.

39.   I bind and cast out all spirits of the dead trailing my life, in the Name of Jesus.

40.   By the blood of Jesus, I renounce and break every oath of allegiance and secrecy made to any secret cult, in the Name of Jesus.

41.   I revoke and reverse all evil decrees and evil judgment against my life, in the Name of Jesus.

42.   In the Name of Jesus, by the blood of Jesus; I destroy every demonic reversal of my destiny.

43.   I renounce and destroy all demonic covenants I entered through my

involvement in evil prayer house, in the Name of Jesus.

44.   I renounce and destroy every concoction I drank there in the name of holy water and oil, in the Name of Jesus.

45.   I renounce and destroy by fire the evil effects of river bathing by evil prayer house prophets or native doctors, in the Name of Jesus.

46.   I renounce and destroy the evil effect of every "saraka" made by me or for me in any form, in the Name of Jesus.

47.   Let the ocean of the blood of Jesus cover and destroy every evil foundation of my life, and set me free, in the Name of Jesus.

48.   Every foundational captivity holding my life, release me by fire, in the Name of Jesus.

49.   I speak into the four corners of the earth, and I command all my held blessings to be released, in the Name of Jesus.

50.   Every agent of Satan attacking my life, jam fire and die, in the Name of Jesus.

PARTNERS

For those who wish to partner with this ministry in anyway, they can write or contact us through this address:

INTERCESSORY ARMY FOR CHRIST

Warmen Control Tower
Opposite Awka slaughter house, (Kwaka)
P. O. Box 1433, Awka
e-mail: warmen54@yahoo.com
web site: www.intercessoryarmyforchrist.org
Tel: +234-8033818084.

Revd. (Dr.) Chima Ugochukwu will like to share in your joy and happiness if the book has been a blessing to you personally or to your Ministry/Missionary work

Use the e-mail address below to send him your testimonies. Indicate if you will like him to add you to his Intercessory Prayer List.

Revd. (Dr.) Chima Ugochukwu
E-mail: warmen54@yahoo.com
Phone: +234(0)8033818084,
+234(0)8181766186.

Printed in Great Britain
by Amazon

82367335R00100